OSBORNE & LITTLE

THE
DECORATED
ROOM

First published in the United States 1988 by
The Overlook Press
Lewis Hollow Road
Woodstock, New York 12498

Designed and produced by Johnson Editions Ltd
15 Grafton Square, London SW4 0DQ

Text Copyright © 1988 Johnson Editions Ltd
Photographs Copyright © Osborne & Little plc
(except where indicated otherwise)

Library of Congress Cataloging-in-Publication Data

Johnson, Lorraine
  Osborne & Little   The Decorated Room
  1. Interior decoration – Handbooks, manuals, etc.
I. Townsend, Gabrielle.   II. Title.   III. Title: Osborne & Little
NK2115. J66 1988   747   87-62140
ISBN 0-87951-304-7

Printed and bound in Spain
by Cayfosa Industria Gráfica S.A., Barcelona

OSBORNE & LITTLE
THE
DECORATED
ROOM

LORRAINE JOHNSON & GABRIELLE TOWNSEND

Principal photography by
Charles Settrington   Fritz von der Schulenburg
Martin Hill
Direction by Felicity Osborne

The Overlook Press
Woodstock, New York

CONTENTS

FOREWORD

Interior decoration has never been more popular. Over this past decade an enormous interest has developed and is reaching a general public previously quite unconcerned with design in the home. Although much more is now written on the subject in books and magazines, this growing number of enthusiastic amateurs is always in need of more reliable knowledge and sources of inspiration.

Like so many other forms of applied art, interior design is fashion orientated. Styles of wall, curtain and furniture treatments continually change and evolve, with novel ideas emerging all the time. But practicality – in the form of cost, comfort and manufacture – is a stringent natural selector and only the best survive to become part of mainstream decoration.

The relationship between old and new is one of interdependence. For without the influence of the new, interior decoration would wither to a museum state, but equally, were it not for the firm foundation of classic design with its tried and tested virtues, innovation would have difficulty taking root. So the two are essential to one another and it is their interaction and fusion that produces exciting, but sound, design.

In this book we attempt to explore a wide variety of design ideas – from general principles through to fine details – explaining briefly their history and offering a guide to their application. We hope that you will try out some of these ideas yourself, take them further and produce personal variations. Because in the end, a scheme that reflects your own taste and individuality is far more rewarding.

We believe that imagination is a key element in interior design. The best and most original results are often produced by an inspired combination of patterns, colours and textures which go beyond the rules. It is that inspiration which lifts the decoration of a room above the merely mundane to become unique and stunning.

Anthony Little

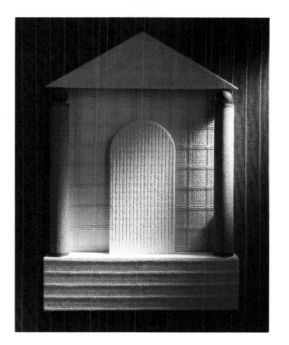

MAKING AN ENTRANCE

The hall should be like the first chapter of a book: it should entice and intrigue, allowing the visitor a foretaste of the style and atmosphere of the whole house without revealing the whole story at once. It should serve as an intermediary between outdoors and indoors and as an introduction to the other rooms, complementing rather than competing with them. The obvious conclusion in decorating terms is that it needs a fairly neutral colour scheme – it is, after all, a functional area: we pass through it on entering and leaving the house and going from one room to another. It also accumulates, inevitably, a certain amount of clutter – another good reason for keeping the background undemanding, to avoid too fussy an effect.

However, neutral need not mean dull. Traditionally, halls have been decorated with painted finishes, such as marbling, rag-rolling and stippling, to give surface interest, all of which can be achieved today with wallpapers. Semi-plain papers are particularly suitable for halls and stairwells as they can accommodate the typically awkward angles and irregular shapes more easily than large patterns. Alternatively, stripes are a perennial favourite for halls and look especially effective in high-ceilinged period houses, as pictures on the following pages show.

Flooring must also be considered, both from the aesthetic and the practical points of view. In the country, tiles or stone flags are ideal: they are hard-wearing and help the visual transition from the outside to the interior. Where carpet is a more appropriate choice, it should if possible be continued into the main rooms leading off the hall; strongly constrasting floor colours glimpsed through doorways can be ugly and reduce the feeling of spaciousness.

Marbled papers are used here to create an impressive setting; its grand architectural effects are *trompe l'oeil,* showing how a featureless expanse of wall can be completely transformed by papers and borders.

Narrow rope twist borders have been cut and mitred to create panels under the 'staircase' and to suggest the line of a chair rail. A blue marbled paper is used inside the panels and below the rail as it appears to recede, reinforcing the panelled effect, while the warmer pink tones of the surrounding areas make them come forward. A wider border imitating a classic cornice with dentils and egg and dart motifs gives a three-dimensional effect under the balusters.

At the window a matching marbled fabric is simply draped over a painted pole, in keeping with the desired classical look.

STRIPING EFFECTS

Stripes are wonderfully versatile: they can be both modern and traditional, crisp and cool, or warm and dark. They are interesting enough to use on their own without further decoration but plain enough to be hung with pictures or allied with panelling.

In the hall of a London flat *(right)*, the effect is light, elegant and restrained. Broad stripes in elephant grey and peach are used to evoke the Regency period and provide a suitable background for a formal arrangement of eighteenth-century lithographs. (Halls, formerly the anterooms or waiting areas of houses, were often used for the display of pictures or sculpture; often works of art would share a common theme, such as mythological or sporting subjects, or, as here, architectural details.) The prints are handsomely presented in uniform mahogany frames with ormolu mounts at the corners, sympathetic in style with both pictures and setting.

The carpet is a neutral, lattice-patterned Brussels weave used throughout the hall, passage and adjoining rooms to achieve a smooth visual transition between one area and another. Lighting is provided by a series of large lanterns – a style traditionally used in porches and entrances to link the exterior with the interior.

Stripes can also be used for a much airier, less formal, look. Here, in pale blue-grey and white, they enhance the high-ceilinged spaciousness of this large hall in a Victorian house *(below)*. The painted panelling is in pale grey, with white used sparingly for the balusters and window frame. The floor has been left uncarpeted, in keeping with the deliberately bare, almost Scandinavian mood, and the boards painted a warm mustard shade to counteract the coolness of the grey walls. But the simplicity of the scheme does not preclude pretty, softening touches: the

curtain, in heavily lined and interlined cotton chintz, is caught to one side in thick folds by a bowed tie-back. The colours – soft blue, mauve and peach – add variety to the large expanse of grey without being too dominating.

In addition, the curving tendrils of the Art Nouveau brass light fitting and the wrought-iron curlicues of the rustic Spanish table balance all the straight lines and hard angles. Flowering plants echo these leafy motifs and help to bring nature inside.

The same wallpaper in different colours sets a totally different mood in the oak-panelled hall on the left. Used here in shades of dark blue it creates a much richer, heavier look. Complete with plaid curtains and stair-carpet, enormous fireplace, dark oil paintings and mock-medieval lamp, the hall's style is authentic Scottish baronial. An imposing Victorian ambience is successfully re-created, but the quirky inclusion of a totally anachronistic model car adds a touch of humour to the Highland gloom and deflates any possibility of pomposity, hinting perhaps that the whole scheme is deliberate pastiche.

Decorating is not merely the choice of fabrics and wallpaper, however: more radical decisions can be made to achieve a chosen look. Here the dark panelling is an essential element and is in fact original, contemporary with this Victorian house. It could, however, have been acquired without great difficulty from one of the many architectural salvage companies. The handsome, massive cast-iron radiator was found in this way and looks perfectly at home in this lofty hall, possessing the old-fashioned solidity such a setting demands.

BORDERLINE CASES

A print wall, reminiscent of eighteenth-century print rooms, has been achieved here *(below)*, by using a combination of two wallpapers and two borders, whose colours harmonize rather than match. As a ground to the ornithological prints, a horizontally striped paper has been used, topped beneath the picture rail by a narrow border with shaded vertical stripes. The same border has been applied at chair rail height, and in both cases has been carefully trimmed to give a scalloped edge. Below this is a pink paper imitating distressed paintwork.

To delineate vertical spaces and suggest the panels that would have framed the images in a print room, a different wallpaper border has been used. A zigzag striped design, it co-ordinates with the ground paper and echoes its horizontal stripes.

An even more original use of borders is shown on the right, where a whole landing and stairwell have been papered with vertical border lengths used back to back to create a striped effect. Obviously, it is not easy to hang borders accurately in this way, but when their design is as striking as this there is a good case for promoting them from secondary importance in a scheme.

In this setting the dominating verticality of the treatment emphasizes the height of the ceiling, and the zigzag effect reflects the shape of the turned balusters. The pattern is continued over the ceiling to unify the whole area and disguise the awkwardly shaped casing at the top of the passage wall. Even the downlighter above the staircase has been camouflaged by two short lengths of the border, so that it merges with the background.

HALL FURNITURE

This large hall, in a mid-nineteenth-century London house owned by collectors of Arts and Crafts pieces, is dominated by its furniture and decorative objects. Thus decoration did not entail elaborate design, merely the provision of an undistracting background. The minimal patterning of the wallpaper resembles rag-rolling and adds surface interest to what are in effect virtually solid colour walls.

The shade chosen is a rich terracotta, a suitable foil to the warm wood tones of the impressive sideboard. Though, of course, intended for the dining room, sideboards are highly suitable pieces of furniture for halls: much more practical than conventional small tables, they are capacious enough to swallow all the clutter that inevitably accumulates in a family house. This fine example in the Gothic style, with ceramic tiles, inlaid wood detail and brass hinges, is by John Pollard Seddon, one of the masters of the Arts and Crafts movement, who also designed furniture and ceramics for William Morris. On the sideboard is a collection of lustreware pottery by William de Morgan.

The chair and settle, in a lighter, less ornate style, are covered in a printed cotton whose geometric, slightly Art Deco design accords surprisingly well with the furniture's delicate angular lines.

Polished floorboards with a nineteenth-century Turkish kelim are right both historically, in terms of the period of the house and its contents, and visually – they lead the eye on to the woodblock floor in the study beyond, increasing the feeling of spaciousness.

Above: Behind the settle is an Art Nouveau screen covered in its original printed velvet. Above it is a Swiss cloisonné panel of the same period. The ruby glass of a huge hall lantern casts a warm rosy glow overall.

REEFED CURTAINS

In the eighteenth and nineteenth centuries France set the fashion for dramatic window draperies. Pattern books, such as Jules Verdellet's *Manuel géométrique du Tapissier*, were avidly studied all over Europe. As the American writer Andrew Downing said in *The Architecture of Country Houses* (1850), 'The French ... have the best taste in the management of curtains, because they have both a natural and a cultivated taste for dress and the arrangement of drapery.'

These two photographs illustrate very different versions of one such eighteenth-century French innovation. 'Reefed' curtains – those that are looped up to one side with cord – can be extremely elaborate or almost medieval in their simplicity. Reefing is an excellent way to show off a piece of beautiful antique textile, such as the Persian painted hanging (*left*).

A much more elaborate version of reefing is shown on the right. Here there are full-scale dress curtains complete with under-curtains. But elaborate though they are, they also have a practical purpose in that they help insulate the room. Lined and interlined, and backed up by silk under-curtains, this treatment gives a rich warmth, both actual and visual, on cold, dark nights.

There are, of course, several different types of heading suitable for a particular style of curtain, but here pinch pleats accentuate the stripe of the fabric. To add to the generous scale of the whole arrangement, a thick plaited cord has been used for reefing and trimming, while weighty tassels and deep fringing give an opulent finish.

BETWEEN INDOORS
AND OUTDOORS

This unusual and striking way of treating an expanse of wall is a remarkably versatile decorating solution. A windowless or featureless hall would benefit from this treatment, as would any room where less than perfect walls make hanging wallpaper or applying paint undesirable. It would also be useful for a passage, making an effective transition between a secluded, possibly dark, interior and the outdoors, and of course would ideally suit a conservatory or sun room where there is usually only one solid wall, the others being glazed.

The softly draped fabric used as walling has been secured at regular intervals – a particularly practical idea, since the length can easily be removed or changed at a whim.

A pretty detail is the way each drape is caught with a simple dark red fabric bow, the same shade being used to band the side and bottom edges of the fabric panel.

As for the fabric itself, its design of brightly-hued crocuses in variously patterned oriental bowls emphasizes the botanical function of this conservatory setting. However, the same treatment would be equally effective in entirely different fabric – imagine the walls of a study draped in a dark plaid or a young girl's bedroom hung in a pretty flower print.

To go with the imaginative wall treatment, unusual furnishings have been selected. Instead of the ubiquitous white-painted wrought-iron furniture one might expect, there is a handwrought chaise longue whose delicate curlicues are reminiscent of the tendrils of climbing plants. Two of the cushions on the chaise (*see detail on the left*) are made from the drapery fabric, piped in a contrasting shade of pale peach, while the one in the foreground features an appliquéd motif of a bowl of crocuses on a stippled peach background fabric. The deep blue squab cushion on the chaise picks up the blue of the bowls – both real and fabric – and the gleaming ceramic vase, while the cool white ceramic tile floor effectively sets off the clear bright colours and is ideally practical for rooms in which plants take priority.

NEXT TO NATURE

Halls are not only the transitional areas between outside and inside; they also bridge the barrier between house and garden, between organized interiors and rampant nature. Bringing plants – preferably large and lush – inside creates an informal garden atmosphere which leads naturally on to the real garden beyond.

A conservatory or garden room is an enormously attractive asset to any house, whether it is used for its original purpose to cultivate tender plants or just as an extra sitting room. Here both the stone-flagged floor of the hall continuing through into the conservatory and the large scented-leaved geraniums on the inner side link the two areas, and the loosely draped swag over the french doors helps to turn the conservatory into a real room. Blue marbled fabric is used for the swag, with pink marbled paper on the walls, the two united by the rope border in both colours at cornice height and the pink bows that pull up the swag at either end.

The glazed roof of the conservatory is shaded by a gathered canopy of translucent white gauze. Beneath it a glorious profusion of climbing and trailing vegetation, roses and lilies, patchwork cushions and old hats create a wonderfully nostalgic setting.

In the other picture the small back hall of a country cottage is not the normal untidy dumping ground of boots, coats and garden tools. Simple but thoughtful decoration makes it comfortable and welcoming. Floor-length curtains in a shagreen print can be drawn across the door to keep out draughts; matching wallpaper is used to avoid breaking up the small area with different patterns. A design such as this, though only faintly patterned, is a more interesting choice than plain paint and makes a better disguise for old and uneven walls.

Coir matting is the warm-looking and practical flooring, its natural texture harmonizing with the wicker baskets and cache-pots. The grouping of plants on the skirted table reflects the greenery beyond.

A PLACE TO DAYDREAM

Few places around the house can be quite so perfect for daydreaming as a window seat. It's the ideal place to watch the weather, contemplate the garden or to read by natural light propped up by comfortable cushions. However, because it is usually a recessed alcove in a hall or landing, its decoration must be considered in terms of the larger setting. Here are four examples of ways to treat a window seat.

In the hall of a Queen Anne country house (*left*), the distinctive shape of the window dictated the style. A pelmet was not appropriate, since the window almost reaches the ceiling and any hanging fabric would have obscured the central arch. An antique mahogany pole with turned ends seemed the obvious solution. Because the pole extends beyond the exact window area, the curtains can be drawn completely back to let in maximum light or allow the wooden shutters to be used instead.

The curtains themselves are in a thick soft velvet chenille, a particularly suitable choice for a hall as it excludes draughts effectively. The curtains, in a welcoming warm coral shade, are made in a simple tailored style with a softly gathered heading; they are edged with a broad ribbon trim in tones of grey, mushroom and ivory, matching the rope and tassel tie-backs. The coral is repeated in the broadly striped wallpaper, whose stripes are in turn picked up by the thick tapestry weave fabric covering the window seat squab cushion. The warmth of the colour scheme is accentuated by further touches of coral in the antique Indian dhurrie and the cushions on the window seat.

The other main colour in the scheme is grey, which appears on the window seat cushion and is also used for the egg and dart moulding, the skirting board and the window panelling, to contrast with and tone down the bright white-painted window frame.

This corner of a study (*right*) is a very personal and peaceful retreat. An unusual combination of apricot and teal blue is used in the room's decoration. Different shades of apricot were chosen for the paintwork around the window, for the tablecloth and for the long cushion, while the curtains are in a predominantly blue glazed chintz. The same fabric is also used for the contrasting thick rouleau trim on the tablecloth, and for cushions on the window seat and wicker chair.

The window seat above, on a landing overlooking a leafy street, shows an ingenious way of curtaining a bay window: the smocked pelmet and outer curtains are fixed, while the under-curtains of blackberry striped silk are the ones that can actually be drawn.

For the window seat on the left, a much more formal note has been struck. The pelmet with its two inverted Gothic shapes has been covered in a pale apricot-striped silk. A contrasting, darker coral stripe has been chosen for the three bowed cravats which hang at the centre and sides of the pelmet. Behind the pelmet, the lower edge of a festoon blind, also in the darked striped silk, is visible. The walls, dado, cornice and panelling are painted in various shades of coral and off-white to tone with the two silks.

TENTED ALCOVES

Whether the idea of covering walls with fabric hangings originated as a disguise for damaged surfaces, as an excuse for using a favourite fabric extra lavishly or just as an instance of early nineteenth-century nostalgia for antiquity – the fabric-draped walls seen in Pompeiian frescos, for example – we do not know.

The idea and its related style of 'tent rooms' appear to have been resurrected in France at the end of the eighteenth century by the decorators Percier and Fontaine, perhaps inspired by Napoleonic campaign tents. By the beginning of the nineteenth century, French decorators working under Henry Holland were creating tented rooms for an English clientèle. Sometimes, all four walls were loosely draped with fabric panels; sometimes the fabric was pleated or ruched. The ceiling was also covered with fabric, either stretched taut and seamed, or gathered into the centre with a sunburst effect. The focal central point would be either a light fitting, a large tassel or soft bunch of gathered fabric called a *chou* or rosette. Often, where the ceiling of the tent met the walls, a shaped valance or pelmet was used to cover the join, giving the effect of a sumptuous circus or Bedouin tent.

In this room the ceiling is treated lavishly, with a camellia-patterned fabric gathered into the central *chou* (*see detail below*), while the valance is also gathered and shaped. The valance is trimmed with a darker stippled fabric, as are the curtains which hang in each corner of the room. However, instead of fabric hanging from the walls, a co-ordinating wallpaper has been used, so the room is only semi-tented.

This would be a good method to choose for a small room with a window, where it would be difficult to use fabric on all four walls.

In the picture above, glazed striped fabric in two co-ordinating widths has been used: the thinner stripe for the softly gathered walling, the thicker stripe for the sofa, ceiling and table (that way round so that the walls are less dominant). The ceiling is smooth, cut into quadrants which meet at the centre in a *chou*. This method – of stretching quadrants taut – is particularly effective for ceilings when, as here, a striped or geometric fabric is used; the romantic gathered treatment on the previous page lends itself more naturally to flowery designs.

Where the ceiling meets the walls, a scalloped valance has been cut so that the scallops are formed from the darker blue stripe. This valance also hides the join between walls and ceiling and covers the fixing used to hold the curtains in place. The designer has used part of the same stripe to accent the piping on the sofa and table. Note how piping is also used to conceal the joins between the ceiling sections.

The silk-covered table lamps have box-pleated silk shades in a creamy yellow, toning with the peach stripe in the curtain fabric. Deep box pleats are also used for the floor-length tablecloth – with a large pattern such as this stripe it is imperative that the pleats are all the same size, so that the repeat is regular. Similarly the upholsterer has carefully matched the stripes on the sofa so that they connect, running from the back, across the seat and down to the valance.

DRAWING ROOMS

PANELLED
IN PAPER

For the walls of this room the owners had to create a background that would not compete with the eclectic mix of interesting furniture and objects which clearly had to take precedence over the décor. (There are examples of Biedermeier and Arts and Crafts alongside Baccarat, Tiffany, Carlton ware and Clarice Cliff.) They chose a sand-coloured wallpaper with an overall grainy pattern, but to make it more interesting they created a panelled effect, echoed in the cupboard detailing, by applying strips of the same wallpaper in a strongly contrasting charcoal colour.

Though the room is large and potentially intimidating, the owners had the confidence to give it an air of elegant informality by mixing fabrics and colours. By covering the sofas in a dark stippled chintz and the arm-chair (*seen in the large picture overleaf*) in a lighter-toned plaid the room is given a cheerful atmosphere that works equally well in winter and summer. (This is an important point to consider when choosing fabrics and colour schemes: there is something uncomfortable about a pastel-coloured room decked out in sprigged cottons in deepest winter, and the same applies to a dark, velvet-draped room in the height of summer. Cotton fabrics in strong, clear colours, on the other hand, look equally right all the year round.) Nor was there any hesitation about mixing patterns: given the proportions of the room the rugs and tapestry cushions blend with the furnishing fabrics without looking too busy or fussy.

The curtain treatment shows the same desire not to let grand ideas overpower family informality. Dress curtains in opulent fabrics can easily look pretentious, so plaid cotton was an inspired choice here, counter-balancing the formality of the draped and swagged valance. This is cleverly arranged to look as though it extends down into the over-long curtains which pool on to the floor, but in fact they are separate lengths. Simple draw curtains hang alongside. Note the covered curtain pole and the cravat marking the central point: by such touches are thoughtful decorators revealed, no matter how much they may have contrived to create a room that looks as if it has simply evolved without any deliberate decorating decisions.

Many fashionable drawing rooms of the Eighties boast a piece of Biedermeier furniture (below): its simplicity of form lends itself particularly well to modern interiors. The Biedermeier style was popular in many countries from about the 1830s, but is most strongly associated with Germany, Sweden and Russia. In essence it was a rebellion against rococo and baroque taste – a simplification of line, a paring down of ornament; blond woods were most often used. Here, a classic Biedermeier settle has been covered in yellow crushed velvet, its formality softened by woven and beaded cushions.

Right: *Another view, with the furniture re-arranged slightly, gives an idea of the room's proportions.*

MING DRAWING ROOM

The drawing room, unlike the informal sitting room, should impress but not intimidate. It is the most important room in the house and so, more than any other, should reflect one's individual style.

The draped pelmet, decorated with stars and rosettes, is the imaginative, indeed fantastic, touch which adds individuality and romance here. Wallpaper of a neat stylized floral in vertical stripes is restrained and makes a good background to the bold oriental print fabric used on the sofa, screen and around the door. Coral and damson-coloured velvet cushions edged in striped cord with frogged corners and a sprigged damson tapestry floor covering complete the soft furnishings. They complement the print and, at the same time, their deep hues prevent it from being overwhelming.

The three-fold pinnacled screen is an extravagant piece of furniture where space is at a premium, but here it is also functional. It adds a feeling of security to the room where the door, with its open fretwork, is more than usually decorative. The triangular side table which fits neatly against the screen is in the same lacquer red as the door and the screen's trim, and echoes the airy oriental style of the door.

A black shaded table lamp on a lacquered pedestal base gives the right subdued atmospheric lighting. The oriental porcelain seat on the carpeted floor adds to the exotic atmosphere. Simple accessories – a bowl of redcurrants, reminiscent of an eighteenth-century still life, and a spray of a formal flower such as this lily – are all that are needed as softening touches.

COOL PASTELS

The sitting room opposite succeeds in solving two common decorating problems: how to combine modern and antique furniture in the same room *and* avoid the tendency of ice-cream colours to look sickly sweet. Antiques may often be inherited or bought on impulse while modern acquisitions are often chosen deliberately to fit into a particular setting, and achieving a harmonious marriage of old and new calls for considerable skill.

In this room, the highly carved chair and pine stand provide the antique touches while the sofa, coffee table and stainless steel up-lighter are more contemporary. The wooden floor is also traditional: before the mid-nineteenth century floors were of stone, brick or wood. Floorboards were often painted, especially if they were made from inferior wood such as pine – here they are of limed oak, giving them a whitewashed look ideal for the room's pastel tones.

The other notable detail is the owner's collection of Art Deco pottery. Its clean lines and soft tones are a bridge between the room's antique and contemporary elements.

The coolness provided by the mint green in the wallpaper also works well with the pottery. In addition, the wallpaper's graduated horizontal stripes echo both the dado rail and the floor boards. (The wall colour below the chair rail has also been carefully chosen to match the palest shade in

the wallpaper's stripe.) To give a modern twist to a classical architectural feature, there is a bold zigzag border in ivory and grey edged by a band of pink. This border also draws the eye to the most unusual detail of all – the curtain rail and rings, hand-stippled like the coffee table to incorporate all the colours in the room. Such attention to detail is perhaps the province of only the most dedicated decorator, but it certainly raises a not uncommon curtain treatment above the ordinary.

Other intriguing details include the shaped tie-backs, edged in the same fabric, with a painted curtain ring to loop over the painted wooden knob. Very long curtain poles have been used so that the curtains can be drawn aside completely when the french doors are opened wide. Finally, after all the careful co-ordination, it is the bold diagonal plaid on the curtain fabric that saves this pastel scheme from looking anaemic.

The same fabric is used to cover the sofa, on which rest unmatched cushions in softly stippled plain fabrics with contrast piping, these plains picking up all the key tones of the main plaid. These same stippled fabrics in pale blue and pale green have also been used to cover the ottoman, chair squab and circular table in the foreground, thus preserving the essential coolness of the room scheme.

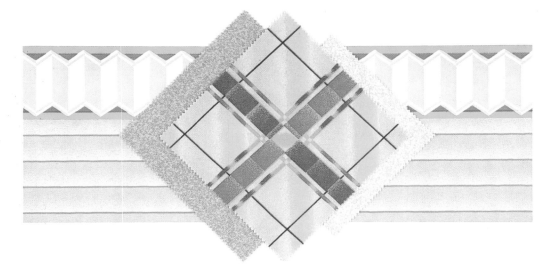

PELMET GEOMETRY

Pelmets – or curtain cornices as they were then called – were originally devised in the eighteenth century to hide curtain rods and rings. How popular they were tended to depend on the fashions in curtain rods: when rods were particularly ornamental there was no need for a pelmet.

Having been out of fashion for a decade or more, due to the preference for Victorian-style brass or wooden rods and rings, pelmets are becoming popular again, sometimes following the Regency fashion for Gothic, scalloped or Vandyke edges, or, as in the main picture on the right, striking a completely modern and innovative note. This geometric pelmet incorporates diamond and triangle shapes to provide an interesting alternative to the usual squared-off style. Here, the points of the diamonds emphasize the vertical stripes of the brightly patterned fabric and direct the eye downwards to the curtains, blind and sofa. To delineate the shapes the geometric panels are edged in a dark maroon fabric.

In the picture above, another modern pelmet has been inspired by the design of the fabric. The mid-blue edging picks up one of the colours in the patterned fabric, and the asymmetric zigzags follow the rhythm of the patchwork pattern. The effect is strengthened by using the same blue along the upper edge of the pelmet. To filter the sun, a roman blind has been hung in the window.

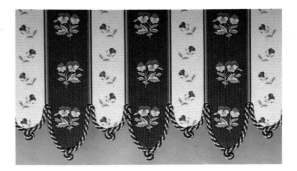

The detail above shows a clever way of making a pelmet from vertically striped fabric. This broadly striped design of pansies has been given a scalloped edge for a banner-like effect, emphasized with rope trim.

COUNTRY COMFORT

There are no spurious folksy touches in the drawing room of this fifteenth-century cottage: the thick stone walls, exposed beams and massive fireplace have so much intrinsic character that attempts at prettifying it would appear trivial. Avoiding the extremes of flowery prints and frilly curtains on the one hand and chilly stone floors and spartan white walls on the other, the decoration relies on textures and patterns to create a welcoming, quietly luxurious environment.

Rather than have the exposed ceiling joists black in the conventional way, they have been painted off-white, together with the boards they support and the window shutters. This maximizes the amount of light available, increasing the feeling of space in this low-ceilinged room. Cottagey clichés have also

been rejected in the choice of wall-covering and upholstery materials. The blue-grey wallpaper has a small beige sunburst motif which tones with the creamy-beige mottled fabric used to cover the fireside sofa. These restrained prints make a good foil to the more colourful elements – the kelim, big squashy cushions and carpet-covered ottoman.

At the other end of the room (above), the blue wallpaper sets off an eclectic grouping of furniture and objects: a Georgian oak sideboard in front of a tapestry panel is flanked by wooden tubs and a hay fork – the only consciously rustic item in the room. Opposite the window an Arts and Crafts armchair stands beneath Victorian prints. The whole room is unified by coir matting extending into the next room; this floor covering is a particularly good base for kelims and other rugs, as it grips them and stops them 'travelling'.

BEAUTIFUL NEUTRALS

The sitting room opposite shows how a room can be utterly contemporary and still use tones subtly different from the 1970's cliché of black, grey, white and chrome. Here a beautifully neutral scheme has been chosen, using several different muted shades. The strong spotted bands of the fabric in mushroom, beige and pewter shades give form to the low, simple sofas and double pouffes in the foreground. The co-ordinating paper with a greyish dot on beige makes an undistracting background, while the border lends architectural interest below the cornice. There is a skilful balance of textural and tonal relationships: without the boldness of the fabric, the sofas would be dull and without the texture on the paper, the walls would be too bland.

Other decisions include the ultra-simple treatment of the windows and cushions. The soft pleating of the unlined roman blinds adds a little softness to an otherwise linear scheme, while the covering and piping for the cushions in stippled fabrics in several different colours provide contrast; in addition, the slight sheen of a glazed cotton works well against the matt colour of the sofa fabric. The co-ordination here derives from the underlying mottled texture of both fabrics.

This exercise in near monotone is completed by the beige tiled floor; the black metal table frames, dark green foliage plants and orange flames in the painting, picked up by the tulips, provide the only contrasting notes in this deliberately restrained interior.

JACQUARD WEAVES

Most woven fabrics today are jacquards. Since their design is integrated into the weave rather than being printed on the surface, such fabrics are exceptionally hardwearing and so particularly suitable for upholstery.

Strictly speaking, a jacquard weave is a fabric woven on a Jacquard loom, a device invented in 1804 by Joseph-Marie Jacquard, a Lyons silk-weaver. Its great innovation was the use of cards punched with holes to 'programme' the lifting of warp threads, making it far simpler and less time-consuming for weavers to produce complicated textured designs. Initially used for the hand-weaving of fine silk brocade and damask, its method was adopted and developed for weaving cotton fabrics on power looms. This has resulted in a process which can create a remarkable range of textures with depth and durability of colour which printing cannot match.

In the picture above, three related wovens have been chosen to create a not strictly matching, yet unified scheme: a thin stripe, a small paisley-type dot, and a larger-scale, interlocking lozenge motif. The lightest hue, ochre, covers the sofa, while the curtains have been made in the darkest shade of brown, so that they recede behind the sofa.

The middle tonal value, that of the stripes, has been kept for the ottoman and roman blind, as these are of secondary importance. The loose cushions on the sofa have been covered in the other two weaves, but they are all piped in the same fabric as that covering the sofa. However, the focal point of the setting is the curtain treatment with its fixed pelmet of points, directing the viewer's eye downwards. Even the tie-backs have the same pointed effect, alternating the dark brown with the ochre.

Again, the darkest and lightest fabrics have been combined for maximum impact, while the middle value of the striped weave, used for the roman blind, recedes.

In front of the sofa, an ottoman makes a practical alternative to the more usual coffee table. Although relics from the Turkish empire, ottomans have several virtues for modern living. Firstly, being essentially covered boxes, they provide valuable storage space; secondly, because the top is usually padded beneath the covering fabric, they have a more comfortable look and feel; and thirdly, they can be recovered repeatedly so that they always co-ordinate.

Because jacquards are also thicker and heavier than most upholstery fabrics, such as cotton chintz, when used for curtains they lend themselves to a more tailored window treatment. At the window above, this quality has been used to full advantage, especially in the geometric treatment of the stiffened and fixed pelmet. The stripe of the pelmet fabric runs vertically to match curtains and covered cabinets but any monotony is relieved by two clever decisions: the ziggurat shape of the pelmet with its three 'steps' on either side, decorated by sewn-on squares of the co-ordinating fabric and the use of the darker co-ordinated fabric for the roman blind.

The fronts of the padded fabric-covered cabinets are enlivened by a criss-cross of brass upholstery tacks (now supplied conveniently in long strips). A self-piped edging has been used to delineate the top.

When choosing such bold treatments, it is essential that accessories are equally forceful – this is not the place for a collection of pretty bibelots or delicate houseplants. All the accessories here have strong, simple shapes, from the celadon vase and antique tin tea caddy to the table lamp with its spattered columnar base and the boldly painted fruit bowl and Art Deco metal tray.

A SENSE OF PROPORTIONS

It is difficult to believe that this room was completely gutted – doorways were re-positioned, a fireplace moved and alcoves resited, and half and full Corinthian columns installed to mark the beginning of the curved window bay – all to achieve the symmetry essential to a classically proportioned room. Moreover, the designer did not stop here in his search for perfection – the colours of the paintwork and wallpaper were taken from a Palladian church in Venice, and even they are not as straightforward as might appear. The cornice is a pale grey, the wallpaper a creamy shade, the woodwork paler than the wallpaper and the skirting board the darkest grey of all, to anchor the room and link it to the floor. The ceiling is not pure white but has been 'dirtied' to avoid glare. The colour scheme is purposely quiet and restrained to be seen in the context of the adjacent rooms,

The detail above shows one of a pair of specially made cabinets, their fronts imitating stonework in a reference to the eighteenth-century architectural prints above.

both of which are decorated much more boldly in deliberate contrast – see the dining room on pages 82–84.

A jacquard weave with a tiny chequerboard design in cool grey and white covers the two matching sofas. For the curtains, with their long tails and graceful swags, a self-striped off-white fabric has been used, the whole treatment finished with a fan-topped fringe. Ottoman and cushions are covered in a tapestry weave, adding rare notes of colour to this pale, neutral scheme. The ottoman is decorated by very deep rope bullion fringe in three contrasting shades.

The fireplace, as the focal point of the room, received the same careful attention. Deliberately plain, it has a black slate slip as the fire surround. Black urns on the mantel shelf and black-framed miniatures are dark punctuation points balancing the black slate, which could have been too heavy in a pastel setting. The fireplace is surmounted by a pedimented mirror, its straight lines relieved and balanced by the curved heads of the alcoves on either side. The wall sconces are hand-carved in lime and painted the greyish stone colour of the cornice.

It is interesting to see the earlier decorative treatment of the same room, replaced by the colour scheme shown on the previous pages. Here a corner is seen with the upholstered furniture covered in darker, heavier colours, with burgundy as the accent against a ground of cream and beige tones for walls, woodwork and carpet. With pattern kept to the minimum, the lines of the furniture are paramount. The settle, based on classic Georgian examples, is a much lighter, more elegant piece than later over-stuffed sofas, which, though comfortable, lack any sense of period style. Four tapestry-covered cushions on the settle add extra comfort. The unusual design of the tapestry weave fabric features a vertical panel of pansies against mock-leopard spots; the same weave covers the ottoman in the foreground. The growing popularity of these fabric-covered boxes is a welcome improvement on the ubiquitous coffee table, which often looks disproportionately low in high-ceilinged rooms such as this.

SWAGGED PELMETS

Elaborate drapery effects come and go, passing in and out of fashion, but it must be said that nothing adds a grand touch more conclusively than generously long curtains, topped by a swagged pelmet. This style, originally conceived during the early eighteenth century, and revived by the Victorians, is popular again today.

However, what has changed over the centuries, and is demonstrated by the rooms shown here, is the belief that this style should be confined to very large windows in lofty ceilinged rooms. For example, in this traditional sitting room *(right)*, the window behind the sofa is fairly small-scale, with no particular architectural merit. Yet the curtain effect makes it the centre of attention in this otherwise restrained scheme.

The pelmet, fixed at the top by a firm heading a few centimetres thick, banded in dark blue-green, has double swags meeting at the centre, the join hidden by a deep fabric loop. Underneath striped curtains hang over a roman blind in a co-ordinating smaller stripe. The same small stripe has been used for the pouffe in the foreground and also for two cushions, which help to introduce the cotton jacquard-covered sofa and side chair. Piping is in the same shade as the banding on the pelmet heading.

Above: For a large window, in a more formal setting, a similarly low-key colour scheme has been chosen. Here, the tails are deeply pleated, but this time double-banded in an accenting blue-green and hanging nearly to floor level. The draw curtains hang beneath a triple swag (although only two are visible here) thrown over the fixed pelmet.

A VICTORIAN PARLOUR

This room, an accurate evocation of the comfortable and confident Victorian age, contains many of its characteristic elements. Probably the most striking feature of Victorian interiors was the depth and strength of colour they favoured – dark shades such as burgundy red, forest green, deep gold, brown and black were popular, even in small rooms. As every student decorator learns, these shades instantly impart cosiness, since they make the walls appear to come forward. Here, peat brown is the background in both the boldly patterned chintz on the walls and the flowery carpet. The chintz has been cleverly hung from another common feature of Victorian rooms – the picture rail. Picture hooks have been slipped at regular intervals through the gathered heading. For further effect, the fabric, which features a large striped ribbon bow holding a trio of variegated camellias, has been cut at the top across a line of these bows to give the impression of a beribboned heading. (See also *Tented Alcoves* on pages 30–32.) Many people are now rediscovering the usefulness of picture rails. Not only do they allow pictures to be hung and repositioned easily without damaging wall surfaces, they also break up expanses of wall.

The curtain treatment is as inventive as the wall hangings: the simple heading is of secondary importance to the vibrant red-orange of the lining fabric.

When furnishing a room in this particular style, some of the conventions of co-ordination have to be ignored. Things should not match, but merely be compatible in a general way. Here there is a mass of pattern upon pattern: the various tapestries covering cushions and the paisley shawl wrapped over the day-bed, the tiles with yellow birds in the fireplace, the carpet and the wallpaper border below the cornice. Nothing matches anything else, yet nothing looks out of place: the cumulative effect is warm and rich.

DARK SHADES

The main picture shows an unusual window treatment combining a fringed swag surmounting cedar slat Venetian blinds. Although these blinds are popular today in both traditional and modern interiors, their history goes back to the middle of the eighteenth century. They are marvellous regulators of light, a quality very much in evidence here as they control the amount of light pouring through this south-facing window and allow the decorator to use a dark, rich colour scheme to great effect.

The room's opulent but comfortable feel is primarily achieved by the lavish window treatment in silk taffeta. The triple swagged valance in bottle green has been edged with a deep rope bullion fringe of sea green and mustard (which also trims the base of the sofa), while a darker shade of mustard appears in the just visible wallpaper. To add a dash of spice, the valance is lined with a bright terracotta which shows only at the pipes and tails. In addition the swag has been crowned with loops of a tricolour rope. Dark shades have also been used for the glazed cotton chintz on the sofa and the crushed velvet tablecloth. The richness is continued by the black-shaded tôle lamp, the plump tapestry weave-covered cushions and orchids in full bloom in the Victorian cache-pot. Here is a perfect example of how dark colours and elaborate design ideas often associated with heavy Victorian interiors can be brought right up to date.

Above: A draped console table gives a rich Renaissance feel to a room, especially as here when it is covered first in crushed velvet and then, with an almost altar-like simplicity, in a check fabric that picks up the grey-blue of the underskirt. The velvet is trimmed with braid while the cotton is finished with a simple binding. The position of consoles against a wall has the advantage of providing a backdrop of wallpaper and pictures for the objects on the table; these should be relatively large and bold – small trinkets do not suit the scale of this arrangement.

FLORIBUNDA

If you are using a big bold pattern in a fairly formal setting, a quite disciplined approach is needed. At this end of a large sitting room, there is no attempt to mix and match designs – the exuberant flowers in the chintz need to be seen *en masse* in all their glory – and the decorator uses the fabric with utter confidence to achieve this delightful country-house effect, although it would certainly be excessive in a smaller room.

In contrast to the lavish window treatment, the upholstery and tablecloth are kept plain and simple – more frills and furbelows would have been too much. Sofa cushions are edged with narrow red piping (made from the same fabric as the trim on the curtains) and the table has a fitted cloth, the angles of the table showing off the fabric design to advantage. Note also how the main floral spray in the design is carefully centred on the sofa cushions and dining chair backs so that they all match – a vital point to remember when using big patterns.

The country feeling is further heightened by the colourful bowls and vases – especially attractive is the grouping of three vases filled with spring bouquets. Other details include the painted chair legs (in off-white rather than dark polished wood), and the trellis pattern carpeting.

Above: *The large window area calls for a positive gesture; here it is achieved with floor-length curtains which hang underneath a swagged pelmet decorated with frilled tails. The tails have deep frills accented with dark red ribbon trim which is also used on the folding tails at each side. This effect needs careful planning – note the symmetry of the design on the two swags and the way the pattern is matched on both tails.*

ROOM FOR THE FAMILY

In a large house with a formal drawing room on the main entrance level there was enough space for another informal sitting room at garden level below.

This is a room for the family, where they can read, watch television and pursue hobbies without constantly having to tidy up papers, books and games. So the idea was to create a mellow and relaxed setting for all these activities.

The wallpaper is a modern abstract design with multi-coloured paint splashes, more contemporary and informal in feeling than conventional rag-rolled and marbled effects. The seats, together with the kelims and tapestry-covered cushions scattered on the floor, are equally informal, and provide plenty of comfortable low-level seating. The seating units are upholstered in a hard-wearing tapestry weave whose design is derived, appropriately, from Turkish textiles – which might well have covered the similar low divans of Ottoman palaces.

Warm colours have been chosen throughout – yellow predominates, with accents of rust, coral and green. All these appear on the walls and seating units, and a strong green has been picked out for the upholstered stool in the window alcove and for the blinds. These have gathered headings curving round the top of the arched windows; when pulled up they fall in loose folds, finishing in handkerchief points defined by deeper green edging. The effect is soft and

Above: *The narrow staircase leading down to garden level is dragged in a complementary warm shade of soft coral. A Clarice Cliff vase and biscuit barrel in cheerful colours, and a child's violin lie on the Victorian gothic marquetry cupboard.*

pretty, in keeping with the view of garden greenery outside. The low coffee table has been specially painted with splashes of colour that incorporate all the various tones in the room.

In complete contrast of scale, the huge Aesthetic Movement bookcase with carved silver hinges not only looks impressive but provides practical storage: the shelves display children's books and contemporary pottery, while the cupboards house games.

COUNTRY LIFE

Country houses, however grand, always look best when their decoration is relatively informal. They need to be warm and inviting and not too immaculate – strictly matching colour schemes and rigid co-ordination are better suited to town houses. But there is a danger of going too far the other way and ending up with a totally haphazard assortment of styles and colours.

The owners of this pretty and comfortable sitting room have been brave in their choice of colours but have not picked them at random: they were guided by the suggestions of the highly patterned chintz used for sofa and cushions. So, while the general mood is chintzy, in the English tradition, unusually bold shades and rich textures add originality. The fabric has broad pink bands with crimson and mustard geraniums alternating with plainer bands of cream decorated with brown dot trellis and blue floral sprigs. Hence the panelling below the dado is painted in shades of blue and cream, and above it is trellis

wallpaper to match the fabric. An armchair in mottled pink (*left*) is piped in mossy green, picking up the geranium leaves of the chintz. The tall ottoman which serves as a window seat is upholstered in a blue tapestry weave, while the china alcove is painted mustard.

To counteract all the blue, which could give a cold cast to the room, reds and pinks have been chosen for the kelim carpet and paisley shawl tablecloth (*above*). Kelims and paisley fabrics, as in the cushions here, are invaluable for adding warmth to a room; when used in conjunction with other fabrics they add an eclectic elegance.

The window treatments here solve a common problem – how to link visually windows of two entirely different sizes. The main window has curtains and a pleated valance with smocked heading – much too heavy for the smaller one. So an Austrian blind with the same heading successfully echoes the valance of the large window.

Above: *Blue flowery sprigs in the wallpaper are repeated in the chintz; blue, in two shades, is in turn picked up by the panelling.*

REVIVING THE LAMBREQUIN

This unusual window treatment is inspired by a style popular in the nineteenth century – the lambrequin, a fixed flat pelmet covered in fabric which extended down the sides of the window, partially concealing plain draw curtains. This fashion superseded to some extent the elaborate draped swags and valances of the eighteenth century. Although owing its provenance to the medieval bed, always enclosed in curtains hanging from a wooden framework, it was eventually transposed to the window, where it was used to conceal pulled-up blinds. In this position, the lambrequin could also be put to another practical use – that of disguising badly made architraves or unpleasingly shaped windows. Today it can still be seen on the exterior of Regency houses, where its purpose was to provide a frame for and protect drawn-up canvas sun blinds. The advantage of using it in interior schemes is that an exotic shape can be constructed from wood which would not be achieved merely by draping fabric; in addition the flat surface allows the fabric design to be shown to full advantage.

Here lambrequins set a mood of formal elegance and dictate the colour scheme – cream and dark blue-green – used throughout the room. The size and shape are determined by the pattern of broad stripes: a pale stripe falls in the centre with full-width stripes at the outer edge. This paler shade makes a visual link with the matching wallpaper, while blue-green stripes frame the curtains.

The dark blue-green shade is also used for the finely striped wallpaper below the chair-rail and for the crushed velvet upholstery of the armchair and sofa, with a lighter shade for the ottoman. This lighter colour is used to pipe the furniture, while a double row of thick green and gold braid round the ottoman completes the colour co-ordination of the upholstery. The same attention to detail extends to the accessories: cushions are in the same print as the curtains, and the lamps have dark blue-green bases and cream shades.

67

CURTAINED CURVES

In decorating circles there has always been some disagreement about the correct treatment of windows. Edith Wharton, for example, writing at the turn of the century in *The Decoration of Houses*, had fixed ideas about the purpose of window coverings: 'The real purpose of the window-curtain is to regulate the amount of light admitted to the room, and a curtain so arranged that it cannot be drawn backward and forward at will is but a meaningless accessory.' Other decorators have regarded windows as opportunities for elaborate drapery, with little concern for the basic function of curtains and blinds.

For the moment, we will side with the latter. Here the symmetry of the central french doors flanked by windows presents the decorator with an unusual problem. The windows are very tall and would require an extravagant length of fabric to make traditional draw curtains; and their round tops, although attractive, make them difficult to dress.

The designer has fitted curved rails well above the window architraves, encroaching on the ceiling cornices. These are hung with a sheer off-white silk, though muslin or thin cotton could also have used. At the door the silk is divided in the centre and swept to each side, while the window lengths are reefed back asymmetrically. This treatment alone would be dramatic yet simple, but the crowning stroke is to top the silk lengths with swags of fabric. The generous swags are gathered up into bunches just beneath the cornice, from which the ends are allowed to hang freely. The tails are symmetrical around the door, but asymmetrical around the side windows, and reach almost to the floor at the outer edges, echoing the folds of the silk.

In this picture ornate portières (door-curtains) in a stippled slaty-blue fabric surmount two internal arches, in a treatment which would be equally successful for round-topped windows. This type of decorative curtain was made in the late seventeenth and early eighteenth centuries and had a brief revival in the second quarter of the nineteenth century. Although fairly common in grand French and Italian houses they were only occasionally used in England – where the first mention of them is in 1691-2 when the cabinet-maker Thomas Roberts charged for making curtain rods for portières in Kensington.

The portières shown comprise divided swags, held back at the sides of the arches with contrasting peach rosettes; over this hang compound swags which have been cut on the bias in two sections to form double sets of folds converging at the centre, while three points on the swag are highlighted by more rosettes. The same peach tint has been used as a lining, and can be glimpsed on the underside of the large tails at the side of the doorway. This design could also be used to soften the sharp angles of a square opening, to echo a window treatment, or to link one side of an opening visually with the space beyond it.

DINING ROOMS

SUMMERY SILK

This dining room in an eighteenth-century country house has all the charm of an elegant summer-house prepared for a fête champêtre. French doors and nearly floor-length windows opening on to a formal garden blur the division between indoors and outdoors; the mossy urn in the foreground, painted panels on the walls and generous piles of fruit on the table all help to bring the garden inside.

Colours have been kept light and delicate to preserve the airy, summery feeling. The wall panels are framed in a soft creamy yellow, matching the dragged legs of the dining chairs, and the design and colouring of the flowers themselves are related to the porcelain on the table. The effect of lighter shades against a darker background was very popular in the 1760s and 1770s: one often finds references to rooms with white drapery hung against coloured woodwork. Similarly, light painted furniture was common in this period, and, as the picture shows, it is an effective way of carrying colour through a room and creating a unified look, avoiding an obtrusive contrast with darker wooden furniture.

The translucent silk curtains frame both the windows and the view beyond, and diffuse the light flooding in from the garden. While the effect achieved by the use of such vast lengths of fabric is lavish and romantic, the actual method of gathering and draping the silk is complicated and precise. Short pleated swags are gathered over a narrow pole. These are in front of draw curtains that fall the full length of the window; they in their turn are in front of festoons. A central knot unites the three different layers. A thicker fabric used in this way would look very heavy indeed, but here the shimmering fluidity of the silk is in keeping with the eighteenth-century lightness of touch evident in the decoration of the whole room.

AN ORIENTAL MÉLANGE

The dining room is an area in which fantasy and a taste for the exotic can be indulged to the full to create a theatrical setting. As guests spend only a limited time there one can achieve dramatic effects which would be overpowering elsewhere. The ambience in this dining room is derived from the Orient, but it is a mysterious, romantic Orient rather than a precise location. John Evelyn, writing in the seventeenth century, an age when notions of geography were less stringent than today, would have called its eclectic style 'Indian', a term he used to cover everywhere from Arabia to China and Japan.

The mélange of oriental elements here recalls the result of another famous Englishman's yearnings for exotic and

adventurous decorations: the Brighton Pavilion, the extraordinary folly designed by Nash for the Prince Regent in 1815. A similar freedom, allowing the unlikely but impressive combination of a mock-Moorish arch constructed from a Japanese-inspired fabric, has been enjoyed here.

The shape of the arched pelmet behind the drapery (*see detail*) is inspired by the *mihrab* (prayer niche facing Mecca) of Islamic mosques, which is the central motif of prayer rugs. It is softened by fabric draped in Regency-style swags, their folds caught up in large *choux*. The octagonal tile shapes in the wallpaper are perhaps also reminiscent of the splendid tiled walls of mosques.

The fabric design is based on Imari vases and plates, examples of which decorate the walls and table. (Imari ware was fine porcelain exported from the Japanese port of Imari from the late seventeenth century onwards. It was richly decorated in characteristic colours of deep underglaze blue, red enamel and gold, with touches of yellow and emerald.) The flower motifs represent favourite symbols of Buddhist mythology.

The modern chairs are *faux* bamboo – wood carved and painted to imitate bamboo in a style much favoured during the Regency vogue for chinoiserie. The table setting suggests an oriental feast in progress – whether in a sultan's harem, a maharajah's palace or a Bedouin tent. The warm, faintly sensual atmosphere created by the decoration is just the effect desired in this dining room.

RUSTIC WARMTH

A striped wallpaper in warm gold and apricot tones is the perfect background to the dark oak dining table and settle in this country dining room. Stripes, first popular in the Regency period, are of course a favourite choice for formal dining rooms but can work just as well in a cottage interior. Here they provide an undistracting background to a collection of china plates and at the same time help create an illusion of extra height in this low-ceilinged room. Both the gold and apricot are picked up by the background of the curtain fabric – a modern botanical design which is overprinted in a soft turquoise and brown.

The small window, deep-set in the thick Cotswold stone wall, is given emphasis by an unusual curtain treatment in which the lining is almost as important as the main fabric. Plain amber is used for a wide border applied at the top and sides and is also revealed at the inner edge. The curtains cross over at the centre and are suspended by ribbon made of the amber fabric from sturdy wooden pegs. They are looped back at the sides with the same ribbon.

A woven jacquard fabric covers the comfortable high-backed dining chairs, its blue and beige toning with related shades in the curtain print.

Above: *The warm golden tones of the striped wallpaper reflect the colours of this early nineteenth-century screen covered in toile de Jouy. Note how the blue-grey painted skirting board unites the blues of the curtains and the dining chair.*

TENTED
IN TULIPS

Napoleon could hardly have anticipated that his influence would extend even to the décor of far-flung rooms. But so it was. Tented rooms came into fashion after the Napoleonic wars when military gentlemen would nostalgically hanker after the adventures of campaign life from within the cosy confines of a room hung with fabric to imitate military tents. Then the ladies adopted and adapted the idea, discarding the military overtones in preference for romantic allusions to the Turkish style.

Today tenting is useful for both practical and aesthetic reasons. On a mundane level, it can hide a multitude of sins, like lumpy walls or years of other people's bad taste in wallpapers. It works best, as here, in a small room – it is, after all, intended to evoke a tent, not a marquee. There are more lavish ways than this to tent a room, with pleated walls and ceilings cascading out from a central rosette; such effects can be seen on pages 30–32. But in this relatively modest country dining room looking out on to the garden a simpler, more rustic effect was desirable.

The fabric, with a design of parrot tulips and grasses, conveys a pretty, slightly countrified and not too flamboyant ambience. Anything too fussy would have drowned the room and created a feeling of claustrophobia, because of its use on every surface.

The pelmet – an element that can be used to great effect in tented rooms – continues all the way round the room, providing a decorative border between ceiling and walls and also hiding the fixing.

Another detail that would add style to any dining room is the table treatment. By having a piece of glass cut to fit the table surface any fabric can be used with impunity as a tablecloth, so that the dining table can really be part of the room scheme.

PASTORAL
POPPIES

For this simply furnished country breakfast room, with its pine table and dresser and sturdy Windsor chairs, wallpaper and co-ordinating fabric with a suitably rustic motif of wild poppies have been chosen. The style of the curtain and tablecloth is straight-forward and unpretentious in order to show off the large-scale design to advantage, yet a few distinctive touches lift the room out of the ordinary. The curtain is hung by means of deep tabs threaded over an old iron pole. It is lined with a toning dark orange stippled fabric which is revealed as the curtain is caught back asymmetrically with a cord attached to the pole – a style deriving from the eighteenth-century fashion for reefed or Italian curtains. The same stippled fabric is used as an undercloth and also for piping round the pleated edge of the chair cushions.

The warm beige background of both fabric and wallpaper blends well with the honey-coloured paving stones. Plain beige is also used in the hall leading into the breakfast room and is tied into the scheme beyond by a narrow wallpaper border in the same colours mimicking fabric braid.

The same fabric used more formally: a stiff pelmet has its lower edge cut in ogees and is edged with fringed braid, also used to finish the inner edge of the patterned curtains.

A WAY
WITH WALLS

In this formal dining room, a vertically striped printed fabric featuring panels of old roses is used for both walls and curtains. Adapted from two original nineteenth-century documents, it is the perfect complement to the antique furniture and collection of oriental china.

Although the use of portable hangings made from Spanish or Portuguese leather dates back to the medieval period, when homes were less well heated and interior walls left rough, the notion of fixed hangings became widespread after the Restoration in England in 1660. However, the use of fabric for covering walls was introduced to England by French decorators in the late eighteenth and early nineteenth centuries. The original English method was to stretch scrim or canvas over a wooden framework fitted to the walls and to cover this with lining paper before the final layer of fabric was applied. Today the technique is used to absorb sound, and add a feeling of luxury. Here the 'bump and stretch' method has been employed, a traditional French technique, which, though laborious, achieves an impressive effect. A thick, soft interlining called bump (or domette) is stretched over wooden battens. Then the walling fabric, which is first seam-joined into the appropriate wall lengths, is tacked carefully over the bump along the lines of the battens.

In modern centrally-heated houses, however, it is advisable to use a linen-backed lining paper to seal the walls before tacking up the bump to prevent dust and dirt being drawn out from the plaster by the warmer temperature on the room side of the fabric. Another important consideration when

hanging fabric on walls is how to cover the tacks or staples used to attach the fabric to the battens. By about 1730 fillets came into use to hide the tacks. These were decorative strips of carved and gilded wood, papier mâché or cast lead. As a less expensive alternative, a plain or decorated braid was used; here a plain blue picot braid has been chosen to pick up the blue leaves of the walling fabric and is applied above the chair rail, below the cornice and round the door architrave.

The warmth of the mahogany dining table, sideboard and turned urns (originally knife cases) is enhanced by the subdued lighting. The only light sources are the carved wood wall lights and the picture light, leaving the room dark enough for the candles genuinely to light the table. The large oil painting with its cornucopia of lush fruit is a particularly appropriate choice for a dining room and its subject is echoed by the planter piled with fruit in the centre of the table. The picture is probably Flemish, one of many similar works produced by unknown artists for foreign customers. The blank area in the centre was left empty to be filled in by a local artist with the purchaser's personal coat of arms or a view of his house.

The china on the table is plain white with a simple silver band, chosen in preference to the more usual gold decoration which would clash with the silver candelabra and tableware. The comfortable dining chairs are upholstered in a blue woven fabric with a small beige motif, the colours toning exactly with the walling fabric.

Above: *Collections of china are an obviously suitable form of decoration for dining rooms and here alcoves originally designed as bookshelves are used to display Imari bowls and plates, their dominant blues and reds reflecting the colours of the roses on the walls.*

STUDIES

STUDIES IN BOLD STRIPES

Libraries and studies are places for reading, writing and quiet contemplation; their decorations need to be correspondingly undistracting, using rich colours but avoiding strong contrasts of light and dark tones. Such discretion need not mean dullness, however. In both these rooms bold fabric designs in strong colours offset the dark walls.

In the picture above, showing a corner of an oak-panelled library in an Elizabethan manor house, the need was for curtaining grand enough for the scale of the room and in keeping with the leaded windows. The broad vertical stripes of the curtain fabric lend themselves well to the diamond-headed design of the pelmet. Long triangles in the curtain fabric alternate with shorter diamonds in a co-ordinating fabric, which is also used for the tie-backs and chair upholstery. Symmetry is essential: note how the red and blue stripes come exactly in the centre of the long triangles, how the central triangle falls in the middle and how the pelmet is finished at each end with a longer corner piece.

In the study on the left the same fabric is used, but in a different colourway, which complements the richness of the mahogany furniture, the floor and wood-grained chimney piece. The co-ordinating wallpaper, a broad stripe in blue-green and dark blue, makes an unobtrusive backdrop to the pictures, leather-bound books and objets d'art – a Chinese horse, and an Imari pot in the same blue tones. The curtains, hung from wooden rings, are deliberately over-long and fall on the floor in heavy folds to keep out draughts. They are finished at the top with a fairly deep fold-over pelmet and drawn back with a simple tasselled cord. The Queen Anne wing chair is upholstered in the same fabric, with seams finished along the wings and arms with traditional brass nailing. The stool and window seat are covered in co-ordinating fabric with a smaller-scale stripe in the same colours and are finished with matching fringed braid. Cushions in old, faded tapestry rather than new fabric are in keeping with the peaceful, timeless mood.

CLUTTERED COMFORT

This corner of a Victorian-inspired study is a good example of how unmatched fabrics can be used as co-ordinates. In this case, two glazed cotton fabrics featuring completely different designs, but with a common lattice theme and similar colours, work together.

On the walls, a pink on buff gingham check is underprinted with the faintest diamond trellis. The co-ordinating fabric (*see below*) used for the curtains features a zig-zag lattice in shades of pink on a blue-green checked ground. However, the decorator decided not to cover the upholstered armchair in the same fabric, but instead picked a more vibrant design, in a burnt red which features a larger and bolder overall lattice pattern.

A similar dark red has been used for a deep pleated ruffle on the curtains and pelmet, edged in a darkish blue-green to pick up the same colour in the border used both below the cornice and above the dado rail. (The crisp pleat works well with the lattice in the wallpaper – a softer ruffle might have looked too pretty.)

The curtains have been made considerably longer than floor length, to amuse by their extravagance and evoke a past, more leisured age. To reinforce the cluttered, lived-in atmosphere of a Victorian room a varied selection of antiques, from the Queen Anne desk and chair to the silver photograph frame, has been included.

In order to accent the moulded cornice, a co-ordinated border with a zig-zag plaid was chosen. Its dark blue-green ground adds the necessary finishing detail to the pale paper, while the darker peach tones work particularly well with the dark-stained wood of the dado rail and fireplace.

A LADY'S SEWING ROOM

The focal point of this comfortable sitting/ sewing room is the luxurious curtaining, which combines glazed chintz and silk taffeta in the amber and blue colour scheme used throughout the room. The striped floral chintz is used for a deep gathered pelmet which reduces the height of the window and at the same time creates a warm atmosphere. This type of drapery recalls the reefed or 'pull-up' curtains of the eighteenth century. Eventually, these curtains became fixed valances, as here, for decoration only, and were used in conjunction with draw curtains. The pelmet is pulled up in symmetrical gathers and is finished at the top by a band of tightly ruched fabric and at the bottom by a gathered frill. The plain blue silk curtains are edged in bands of the striped chintz in authentic eighteenth-century fashion; often patterned fabric was only obtainable in small pieces and so was mounted on plain fabric to make it go further. Unlike today, when fabrics are available to order by the metre, it was impossible then to acquire a specific quantity of fabric; much ingenuity went into making the best use of whatever materials were available.

The patterned fabric is also used to cover the armchair – note again the need for careful planning when using striped fabric so that the position of the stripes matches on each arm and falls symmetrically on the back and seat. The predominant tones of blue and amber are picked up in the cushions, which are made of quilted silk taffeta with padded edges outlined in red braid.

A co-ordinating blue wallpaper picks up the same floral motif as the blue stripe of the chintz. The obelisk lamp has a base spattered in blue and tan and topped with a finely pleated amber silk lampshade.

A GOLDEN GLOW

Mottled gold and amber are the warm and luxurious tones chosen for this mellow traditional study, the whole scheme being inspired by the colour of the bird's-eye maple desk. Dress curtains that emphasize the height of the imposing window are in a deep amber cotton print, reefed with double ropes over a pair of finely striped red draw curtains. The pelmet, an eye-catching feature, has been criss-crossed with a narrow picot braid in a diamond pattern, punctuated by brass studs. The top of the pelmet has an unusual box-pleated heading which has been padded to give a full effect (*see detail below left*). The desk chair is of carved wood painted in a light beige to imitate bamboo, a modern copy of the chinoiserie style first popularized by Chippendale. The thin squab cushion is in striped silk.

The wallpaper, with its soft golden tones and large-scale pattern of a flower entwined with a curling ribbon, is based on an eighteenth-century French design. The top and bottom edges of the papered area have been trimmed with a double border in tobacco and charcoal to give a defining accent (*below right*). The ceiling paper is star-studded – a traditional ceiling motif.

The sofa, chairs and ottoman (*see overleaf*) have been covered in a tapestry weave fabric featuring a small random flower motif on a charcoal ground, which makes a pleasing contrast with the predominance of the warm gold tones.

With a colour scheme such as this, the room is seen at its best in winter, when the fire in the grate is lit to provide both visual and actual warmth. Such strong colours might have been oppressive and inhibiting in a drawing room, but succeed very well in making this study peaceful and intimate.

KITCHENS

COOL, CALM AND COLLECTED

This kitchen/dining room breaks one of the golden rules of ergonomic planning but the success of the room results from this very transgression. The space is long and narrow, and had originally been split into cooking and dining areas with an eye-level divider. However, as there is no other room of the house that could be used as a dining room, the present owners decided to return the room to at least some of its former glory as a dining room. So, as the long wall can accommodate all the necessary appliances and storage even though it means the working area is extended rather than compact, the room has been opened up to double as both family kitchen and civilized eating area. To that end kitchen paraphernalia is kept to a minimum, and the display is of crockery rather than pans. Other items appropriate to a dining room are the French wrought-iron chandelier and cushioned bentwood carvers.

The table runners are made from a cotton fabric softly striped in green and yellow, which has also been used to cover the loose cushions on the hard seats of the bentwood carvers. The runners have been pointed, then fringed with the same linen fabric that hangs at the window (see overleaf).

White was chosen as the principal colour for decoration both to reduce the prominence of the kitchen appliances and to enhance the colours of the china on the open shelves. The predominance of white also means that any colour used in the table setting is particularly effective. But the effect here is far from being cold and clinical. Although the table, faced in bright white plastic laminate, is uncompromisingly square, its sharp angles and gleaming expanse are balanced by the curved lines of the wooden chairs and the graceful loops of the chandelier. The warm tone of the light oak floor also helps to counter the coolness of so much white, while flowery plants and bundles of herbs hung up to dry are further softening touches.

Pale shades of yellow, blue and green have been used for the table runners and all the soft furnishings. Blue and green also feature in the antique corner cabinet and in the panels of stained glass in the large window.

For the window treatment, a loosely-woven, slubbed linen fabric has been cut to a handkerchief point and self-fringed. It not only reinforces the country atmosphere of the room but also obscures the rather bleak outlook. The cut-away lower corners also allow the pretty Victorian etched glass panels to be seen. The same handkerchief points have been used at each end of the table runners, which have also been fringed in the linen fabric.

Left: In keeping with the predominantly white scheme, the original window shutters and a Lloyd Loom sofa have been painted white. In fact, the ubiquity of white in this room allows even the palest of shades to stand out – such as the soft stripes on the upholstery and the blue on the inside of the antique corner cupboard.

A WARM WELCOME

This family kitchen/breakfast room is a wonderful demonstration of the welcoming qualities of a warm-toned room scheme. The golden browns of the antique pine furniture complement the predominantly yellow effect of the whole, heightened by the early morning sunshine.

The room has no eye-catching architectural feature and so could easily have been rather dull. It is the careful attention to details that avoids this. Notice, for example, how a border is used to distinguish walls from the ceiling. In this case, the border is architectural in feeling, imitating a dentilled cornice. The border has also been used in the hall and above the stairs (*below*) to provide a linking element in the decoration.

The colours of the border work well with the plaid fabric used for the curtains and the squab cushions on the dining chairs. And, in turn, both have inspired the design of the ceramic tiles above the sink area in which three colours from the plaid appear on the perimeter border of each tile.

The brass catches of the french door and the rise-and-fall mechanism of the light fitting above the table are further small details that add a traditional feel to what is, in terms of appliances, a thoroughly modern kitchen.

PRETTY AND PRACTICAL

Opinions have always been divided about the practicality of curtains in the kitchen. On one hand it is argued that they are out of place because they get too dirty or are dangerous near the stove; on the other, they can add a much-needed dash of colour or soften the look of too clinical an environment. But today kitchens are often not just rooms where food is prepared but rather multi-purpose living rooms, containing eating, sitting and working areas for all the family. In this case there is no need to treat their decoration very differently from that of any other area of the house. So blinds and curtains can be considered as much a part of the kitchen as of the drawing room. That said, it would obviously be foolish to hang flapping curtains near the stove or sink.

In the small picture prettiness and practicality combine in a simple roman blind in an exuberant floral print which pulls up clear of the sink. (Fabric for blinds can be treated with spray stiffener which gives some protection against dirt and creates a surface which is easy to wipe down. Alternatively blinds made from non-treated fabric can be dry-cleaned, so it's a good idea to see that they are put up in a way that is easy to take down for cleaning.)

In the other picture full-length curtains in the same print are used to frame a large window and to define a pleasant sitting area. The generous fullness of the curtains, caught in by simple tie-backs, and the deep gathered pelmet create a relaxed dining atmosphere.

As an alternative to a picture rail and to lower the apparent ceiling height, a wallpaper border has been used. In tones of soft blue and pale pink, it complements both the fabric and the dragged kitchen cupboards. The cupboards, with their panelled doors, fretwork panels, turned spindles and ceramic knobs, are designed in traditional country style. Storage at the other end of the room is provided by a dresser in the same style, rather than by more built-in units, in keeping with the sitting/dining function of this area.

A COLLECTORS' KITCHEN

This very large kitchen/dining room shows how successfully modern and antique elements can be combined in a single living space. The key to the harmony of the design is the wallpaper – broad stripes for a large square room, in shades of warm cream and blue-grey. Stripes have long been one of the most popular design themes. Their period associations make them a fitting choice for this high-ceilinged room with its Victorian cornice and equally a good foil for the late nineteenth-century antiques which lend so much character to the room. In the background is a striking Aesthetic Movement sideboard by J. Moyr Smith. The mirror, from the same period, is bordered with Minton tiles depicting the seasons.

At the same time, the bold width of the stripes and their warm colour are undeniably modern and in keeping with the dining table and chairs. The table was originally designed to be lacquered but with small children in the family the owners decided that a layer of very fine melamine would be more practical. A

band of wood inlay in two colours, bordered by strips of brass, runs round the sides of the table top.

The striped theme is continued in the window treatment. An unlined fabric is used for a wide softly-gathered festoon blind which is an excellent way of coping with the problem of french windows and shutters. The blind can be let down in the daytime to give shade without cutting out daylight altogether or can be pulled up so the doors can be used freely. Pulled up they form an attractive draped pelmet which softens the angularity of the room and also allows the shutters to be closed at night.

Above: In the kitchen area the units have been dragged on the frames and marbled in the panels in blue-grey to match the wallpaper. Skirtings and window frames have been dragged and shutter panels marbled in the same colour to tie in the kitchen units further. On the top of the blue-grey tiled island unit and on the shelf at the side is a selection of colourful Art Deco china.

DINING OFF THE KITCHEN

When a kitchen forms part of the dining room it cannot be considered only from a functional point of view. Decoratively, it must be considered as part of the larger area, which means avoiding elements generally regarded as practical and appropriate for a kitchen if they are unaesthetic. Here, the cooking area is linked to the eating area by a handsome wood-block floor and a festoon blind made from the same material as the curtain. The blind is edged with scarlet binding to match the roller blind underneath. Smocking along the top of the blind effectively balances the decorative weight of the festoons, as well as providing a pretty detail when the blind is down. To avoid the fussy, feminine effect that festoon blinds can have, a geometric fabric in fairly strong, masculine colours has been chosen.

Although the two parts of the room are visually linked to make a harmoniously unified impression, an oriental screen can be unfolded to block off the view of the kitchen area when required.

Tie-backs are not only useful in holding the folds of the curtain back to let in more light;

they also provide an opportunity to add contrast to the curtain (*see above*). Here a plait of scarlet fabric breaks up the large expanse of print. The curtain is edged in the same scarlet.

Above: *This is a room where detailing counts. The skirting board is marbled in deep, strong colours to tone in with the dark check of the curtain fabric, which is also used to cover the curtain pole. The frame of the french windows is lacquered in brilliant scarlet, matching the tie-backs and trim of the curtains. The same shade appears in the cut velvet chair seat.*

INSPIRED BY CHINA

To show the collection of old English tableware – the main feature of this kitchen – to best effect, other colours had to be kept to a minimum and any pattern had to be very restrained. As both wallpaper and blind fabric are printed on a white ground and feature simple blue oriental figures, they make an interesting but unobtrusive background to the patterned plates.

Equally, everything else in the room is kept light, plain and simple. White-painted tongue-and-groove boards line the backs of

the shelves, the cupboard doors below are absolutely plain, and the modern scrubbed pine table and white stick-back chairs are basic and functional.

This treatment does not make the room 'cold' because the large window admits sunlight almost all day. And in keeping with the overall simplicity there is a plain roman blind, to avoid distracting billows of curtain fabric. The shaped lower edge of the blind is the one softening feature, while the dark blue banding provides the final finishing detail.

BEDROOMS

FORMAL
FLORAL

Floral wallpapers always emphasize the feminine nature of bedrooms, but allied with too many frills and flounces the effect can all too easily degenerate into fussiness.

This room, however, demonstrates how a floral print wallpaper can be used as the basis for a formal and elegant scheme. The repeated stylized camellia motif is quite disciplined, and the pattern is further controlled by a frame of dragged paper fillets at the corners of the room and below the cornice. The dark charcoal grey background of the paper provides a masculine slant and is a suitable foil to the black and white architectural prints. Grey, in a lighter shade, is also used for the silk tablecloths, their natural sheen creating a sculptural effect of highlights and shadows.

Above: *The grey-green bedside lamps, mounted on black marbled plinths, have simple pleated raw silk shades. A pile of books provides an easy way of adjusting their height to throw light at the right angle for reading and to illuminate the details of the prints behind.*

The main fabric is another silk – a striped taffeta in ivory and grey-green. Silk in itself gives such an immediately opulent feeling that it needs to be used with restraint: elaborate swags and ruffles would have looked merely vulgar. Thus the bedcover is quilted in a simple diamond design and the curtains are relatively plain in style. A positive note of colour is introduced by the bright coral silk lining, also used to edge the rosettes which hold the curtains back. There is a hint of this same coral in the variegated leaves of the camellias in the wallpaper.

The judicious use of four different types of trimming adds elegance to the decoration. The bed coronet is decorated with a pinch- or butterfly-pleated heading, trimmed with double fan edge braid, while the box-pleated valance below is edged with a deeper fringe. A fringe would not be suitable for the vertical leading edges of the bed curtains, however, so a narrow single fan edge braid has been used.

Another view of the room (*left*) shows the window treatment: plain draw curtains are in the same striped silk as the bed curtains, and the pinch-pleated pelmet and curving valance repeat the design of the bed coronet.

A corner fireplace can be difficult to assimilate into a room scheme, but here it is treated almost as a piece of furniture, painted to imitate stonework in beige tones to match the paper fillets. The fireplace recess is lined and edged with Delft tiles, and the chimney breast is decorated by a collection of blue and white Chinese pots.

CHINTZY CHESTNUT

An English country house is the natural habitat of flowered chintz. Here the light and airy main bedroom has been decorated with a multi-coloured fabric and co-ordinating wallpaper with a design of chestnut spears. The choice of this colourway, in which mauve and blue predominate, was unusual, as these can be particularly challenging shades to accessorize. It was decided to emphasize them, however, by picking the deepest purple for the window seat cushion, the largest expanse of solid colour in the room (*below*). The cushion fabric has a fine navy stripe which tones well with all the bluish mauve elsewhere.

The background of both fabric and wallpaper is a creamy lime shade, and this has been chosen, together with a putty tone, for the painted panelling and fireplace rather than pure white, which would have been too stark a contrast.

Another strong colour – the ginger shade present in the fabric – is used to edge the curtains and in the thick twisted rouleau tie-backs. Antique bead and carpet cushions on the window seat combine all three strong tones – navy, purple and ginger.

The window, with its Venetian-inspired Queen Anne curve, reaches almost to the ceiling; rather than obscure its pleasing shape and cut out light by using a pelmet, a plain brass pole was used to hang the curtains, which have a gathered goblet heading.

A COLONIAL FANTASY

In our bedtime fantasies who among us has not imagined lying languidly in tropical heat, the bed swathed in yards of mosquito netting, listening to the chattering of lemurs and the cries of exotically plumed birds from the faintly menacing jungle outside? Here oriental elements – the bedhead, fabric design and accessories – are combined with occidental – the luxurious bedlinen, quilted bedcover and wallpaper design – to create a setting that is both extraordinary and alluring.

Most of us, whether from inexperience or timidity, shy away both from using such strong colours and from fulfilling secret dreams about what we want a room to be. But here unusual decisions and strength of vision show how successfully such a dream can be realized. The exotic nature of the setting is emphasized by the contrasts within it, the most striking being between the delicacy of the bamboo grove on a painted panel in the background and the boldness of the chintz. Note how the motif of the navy and white vases filled with vibrant variegated peonies

stands out against the chocolate brown back ground of the chintz, and how the darkness of the chintz contrasts dramatically with the white sheer silk drapery. Without the knotted and draped chintz canopy the white would look too cold and formal, but as it is, the chintz is caught into a large loose knot at the top to create utterly inviting surroundings.

The wallpaper complements the chintz, with the same peonies scattered over a buff ground. More European than oriental, this design recalls the floral borders of eighteenth- and early nineteenth-century printed cottons from Mulhouse in France.

Other decorating details in keeping with the oriental theme are the painted wooden floorboards, the pile of pillows and, of course, the urns and bowls, with monkeys and pheasants adding a daring theatrical touch.

An ingenious and dramatic setting, this bedroom shows what can be created by letting imagination indulge itself to the full.

BOLD BORDERS

Often borders are used as discreet finishing touches to frame the design of a wallpaper or in place of a cornice between wall and ceiling; usually the wallpaper itself is dominant and the border a mere accessory.

However, this bedroom shows how effective a border can be when used as the focal point of a decorative scheme. The floral band used here is extra wide and is teamed with a wallpaper in much paler pastel tones which act as a background. The scale of the room is large enough to allow use of the border not only at cornice level, but also above the skirting boards and vertically at the corners. The large window provides scope for a generous sweep of the matching fabric for full-length curtains with a deep gathered

undulating pelmet, giving a soft informal effect. The pelmet falls in loose tails at the sides, showing the same pink lining as on the curtains themselves. A toning pink is used for the upholstery of the sofa seen in another view of the room (*opposite, below*). The ottoman at the end of the bed is covered in the same floral fabric as the curtains, but to avoid an excessively co-ordinated look a number of mixed decorative elements are included in an uninhibited spirit – the painted Victorian Gothic headboard and dressing table, antique patchwork quilt, oriental rugs, colourful cushions, American Arts and Crafts chair and antique mirror – the whole being brought together and framed by the dominant pattern of the border and curtain fabric.

The same border, just visible through the double doors, links the bedroom to the adjoining bathroom (below). Paisley and tapestry-covered cushions on the sofa and lacquer boxes on the low table add to the profusion of pattern.

Another view of the bed alcove (left) shows the wonderfully ornate headboard in the style of Burges and above it a Pre-Raphaelite painting framed very effectively by the floral border.

CAMELLIAS
AND RIBBONS

This bed is reminiscent of the romantic
bedrooms of the eighteenth century when
beds were crowned with canopies bedecked
with acres of fabric and miles of trimmings.
Some of these were influenced by the ideas of
Daniel Marot, a Huguenot architect
(c. 1660–1752) working in Holland and
England, who was the first to produce designs
not only for architectural decoration, but also
for co-ordinated furniture and upholstery.
Here, a simpler but still impressive corona
hangs above ruffled cushions and a deep
buttoned quilt.

The corona itself is gathered simply at the
top to form a soft ruffle and finished with a
soft rosette. The curtains are drawn back at
each side of the headboard and fastened by
more rosettes to reveal a lining of self-striped
silk in a deep aquamarine. This colour plays
an important part in saving the room from
being too sweetly feminine, and picks out the
darker tones in the flowered paper and fabric.
Note that the same silk has been used for all
'secondary' items such as the covered
headboard, valance, tablecloths and blind.
The dark tone and texture of the stripe
recedes against the bright camellias of the
wallpaper and the main fabric, which has
been used for the other soft furnishings of
primary importance such as curtains, quilt,
ottoman and window seat. It takes some
decorating confidence to use a stripe together
with a floral motif, but this scheme is
evidence of how well it can work.

An effective detail is the use of a deep red
for piping and edging the ruffled cushions,
repeating the colour in the variegated
camellia petals. This same red is seen in the
pleated lampshades and over-tablecloths.
Another revival is the eiderdown on the bed,
out of fashion until recently, but looking just
right here with its tiny covered buttons
creating a feeling of old-fashioned comfort.

AN ENGLISHWOMAN'S BEDROOM

Here is the epitome of the Englishwoman's bedroom – crammed with family pictures, mementos and *objets de vertu* and decorated in soft colours and floral chintz. Very much a personal retreat, it is dedicated to comfort and indulgence, so much so that one wonders whether its fortunate occupant ever chooses to read or rest in any other room.

The predominant tones are cream and peach: cream for the walls and the background of the fabric, peach for the door panels and cornice, the bedhead and bed curtain lining. The main floral fabric used for the bedcover and armchair has been outline-quilted to give a feeling of softness and luxury. The bed canopy is topped by frilled swags falling from a curved pelmet which

follows the design of the cornice. The bed is further decorated by a collection of cushions, some large and functional in quilted cotton or tapestry, some tiny and purely frivolous in satin and lace.

The large picture shows the pretty window treatment which unites the bay windows into a single sweep: floor-length draw curtains in the same fabric as the bedcover and armchair are surmounted by a continuous valance caught up and pleated at the top at regular intervals and finished by a double ruffle along the lower edge. The quilted day-bed piled with more lacy cushions is a positive invitation to ring for tea and then sink back with an absorbing book into its welcoming upholstered depths.

JAPANESE MINIMAL

This sophisticated version of a Japanese fisherman's hut is an inspirational evocation of one of the most minimal interior styles in the world, currently as much in vogue in the West as in the East.

Although no obvious decorating clichés immediately strike the eye, in fact some very careful decisions have been made to preserve the clean geometric lines and functionalism essential to the Japanese aesthetic ideal. For example, the curtains on the four-poster are not gathered in the normal manner, but rather hung from broad, plain loops which fall into wide, smooth box pleats. Then there's the bed itself, made from square posts in rough dark wood lashed together with cord in the simplest possible fashion. The bolster, a plain cylinder, adds to the ascetic mood.

The colour choice, too, contributes greatly to the overall impression of cool simplicity. The palette is restricted to blue and white, the familiar colours of oriental porcelain, which also have suitably nautical

associations. The design of the chintz itself is a modern interpretation of traditional scenes of stylized pine trees, figures in boats, waterfalls, bridges and bamboo groves – images borrowed from embroidered hangings, porcelain and lacquer screens. The wallpaper has solitary figures of fishermen casting lines and carrying fish baskets, based on the drawings of Hokusai, whose nineteenth-century woodcuts and illustrations are so amusing to the European eye. Both fabric and paper have a lot of white space, keeping the whole effect very light.

The white-painted floorboards and wooden frame of the wallpaper panel evoke the interior of Japanese houses with their sliding paper partitions, and give the impression that one can step outside into an idealized landscape with a jetty zigzagging across the sea into infinity. This illusion is created by a back-lit paper panel; as a window treatment it would be an ingenious way to disguise a bleak outlook.

A CELEBRATION OF CHINTZ

For the last three hundred years, chintz has been a popular favourite for soft furnishings. The term derives from the Hindi word for 'spotted', but has come to mean a glazed cotton fabric, usually with a printed design of flowers, birds or landscapes.

The European fashion for Eastern-printed cottons began early in the seventeenth century. However, imports of *toiles des Indes*, as they were called, were very restricted, until a Monsieur Oberkampf began producing imitation toiles at Jouy in France in 1760. Toile de Jouy traditionally had the design printed in one colour on white, while chintz in England soon became multicoloured. Oberkampf's early designs were simply imitations of the oriental cottons, but it was not long before a curious mélange of Chinese pagodas, French landscapes, Italian grottoes and classical motifs were blended together, and indeed these combinations can still be found on modern toile de Jouy fabrics.

Apart from the visual appeal of chintzes, they have practical advantages: the glazed finish helps them wear well and resist dirt.

In this bedroom, the glory of chintz can be seen to full effect. At the fireside (*above*), huge peonies spill over a skirted chair, tablecloth and frilled Austrian curtain. There are some special touches: note that the flowerhead has been centred at the top of the chair, while the gathered skirt falls just to floor length.

This tablecloth style is repeated for the bedside tables (*left*), while the bed is very simply covered but crowned by a splendid canopy, made by cutting lengths of chintz on the bias and draping them from the large double *chou* at the top. Underneath, more cut-on-the-bias folds of creamy cotton also radiate from the top, and are caught at either side of the bed by more double *choux*.

The absence of a central lighting fixture contributes considerably to the restful mood of the room. Illumination comes from the bedside lamps (their box-pleated shades in undyed raw silk giving a particularly flattering light), from the glass-shaded Art Nouveau lamp on the fireside table and from the warm glow of the fire itself.

NON-SEWN CURTAINS

This peaceful and essentially contemporary bedroom was inspired by elements from oriental interiors – a simple low bed with bolster and a low table with cushions piled up for seating.

The curtains are very unstructured with just two large squares of a plaid, lined and edged in a stippled mossy green, draped unsewn over a bleached wooden pole creating an informal banner effect.

This same plaid, which is underprinted with softly graduated stripes to add dimension and texture, is also used for the cushions and bedspread. The walls are covered in the co-ordinating paper which has stripes softly blended as in a rainbow, recalling, incidentally, printing techniques pioneered in the eighteenth century. A matching border, with this time a diagonal stripe, accents the simple ceiling mouldings. A semi-glazed cotton in a pale golden tone has been used for bolster and bedspread, quilted with parallel lines echoing those on the plaid. And just to add a little surprise a deeper-hued plaid in a diamond check to contrast with the main fabric has been used for the small bed cushion.

Piping plays a significant role in this scheme. In order to make a feature of the bed and accentuate feelings of ease and comfort, cushions, bolster and quilt have very thick wadded rolls as piping. Then deliberate colour choices bring the room together as a whole: the same moss green stipple edges the pelmet and all the cushions, while the main plaid is used to edge the bolster and quilt.

Functional and sympathetic objects such as the pale wooden steamer chair, raffia baskets, hand-carved wooden bowl and reeded mirror complete the scene. A finishing touch is the coffee table which has been painted with criss-cross brush strokes in a plaid that incorporates all the different tones of the soft furnishings.

Above: Should a more formal window treatment be desired, traditionally-styled curtains could be made from the same plaid, perhaps with a deep pleat overlap at the top. If early morning light is a problem, use the same stippled fabric as the bedspread for the under-curtains interlined with blackout. Tie the over-curtains back with a double plait made from the plaid and the plain material, as the detail above right shows.

THE WELL-DRESSED
DRESSING ROOM

An otherwise ordinary room becomes exceptional when the owner's personality comes through. In this dressing room, decorated in French Empire style, the masculine tone is set by the classic lines of the Biedermeier day bed and the rich, dark colours of the wallpaper and soft furnishings. The tortoiseshell wallpaper, executed in rich reds and black, has been overlaid with strips of amber paper with a small green floral and dot motif (see detail). These criss-crossed strips appear both above and below chair rail height, and are reminiscent of the style of decoration with a Roman military theme beloved by Napoleon and revived after the French Revolution. The drapery over the bed heightens the effect of a military campaign tent, as does the rather extravagant curtain treatment. Swags of striped silk were extremely popular in the early 1800s in France – perhaps in imitation of the striped bunting which was hung on buildings to celebrate Napoleon's victories. The ropes which fix the tails of the curtain arrangement and finish as tricolour tassels further reinforce the military theme. Ropes and tassels are often indispensable to important curtain treatments such as these; they add a strength and authority which no amount of more detailed curtain-making techniques,

such as tucks and folds, can match. However, to balance the military theme, the fabric used for the curtains and the outer bed drape is a glazed chintz featuring Chinese red lacquer pots filled with peonies.

The curtain pelmet has an unusual detail – it has its own cornice, covered in the same chintz. This method, first seen on early state beds, of softening hard-edged mouldings with fabric covering is particularly appropriate to bedrooms.

A LONDON EYRIE

A small guest bedroom at the top of a London house provides an immediate welcome with its lavish window treatment, luxurious padded headboard and quilted bedcover.

A strié wallpaper in mushroom has been chosen as a neutral background to the chestnut print chintz and is given definition by a narrow multi-coloured wallpaper border whose tones – dark brown, mauve, blue and ochre – pick up the main shades of the chintz. The mauve appears in the painted cornice and the brown is used as a finishing touch on the curtain valance. The decorative curtains cannot be drawn because of the projecting radiator grille and so are permanently held back by thick plaited tie-backs in a toning brown. The functional part of the curtaining is the softly draped Austrian blind; the deep curved pelmet is finished at the bottom with a brown-edged frill and at the top by another thick plaited brown band which carries on the darker shade of the wallpaper border. A second strong contrasting colour – deep pink – is used for the frilled lampshades and, in an even richer tone, for the crushed velvet bedside tablecloth to add a piquant note to a scheme that otherwise might seem too pretty.

The pattern of the chestnut spears on the chintz is emphasized by the outline quilting of the bedcovers. These have a scalloped edge repeating the curve of the headboard, blind and pelmet. The avoidance of sharp angles and hard surfaces adds greatly to the comfortable feeling of this room.

A close-up view of the bed cover (above left) *shows the outline quilting of the chestnut spears and the reverse side in stippled mauve. The same shade of brown is used for the plaited band below the finely pleated pelmet heading as for the narrow edging of the frill* (above right). *It also ties in with the wallpaper border beneath the cornice.*

A ROMANTIC FOUR-POSTER

In the seventeenth century it was customary for the aristocracy of Europe to receive guests while seated in bed. Hence, the bed became the principal item of furniture in noble apartments, so justifying ornate decoration. Sumptuous four-posters originated in the Renaissance, although even quite humble beds were enclosed as early as the fourteenth century for practical reasons – to protect the sleeper from chilly draughts and, as bedroom windows were often uncurtained, to exclude light. However, by the seventeenth century, heavy brocades and velvets had largely given way to lighter linens and cottons, partly for reasons of hygiene and partly as a result of printed cottons being imported from the East.

The romantic four-poster has come back into fashion, although the purpose of its curtains is decorative rather than functional in today's centrally-heated houses. Nothing can make its occupant feel quite so pampered as a lavishly curtained bed, even if the curtains are no longer drawn; indeed, as the picture shows, you do not even need a real four-poster to create the right effect. You could either suspend a rectangular frame over the bed and use that as the canopy or simply hang the curtaining and pelmet from the ceiling itself.

For comfort, this bed has a padded headboard, edged with turquoise piping and wonderfully soft for propping pillows against and settling down with a good book. Then there are several unusually luxurious touches: the quilted outline of the striped roses in the chintz; the thick rouleau edging and overlong cloth of the bedside table, and the flowing lengths of the same chintz at each corner of the bed tied back with long banded ties. Turquoise piping throughout unifies the various elements and a softly marbled yellow wallpaper and upholstered stool show that an unobtrusive design can provide a foil to the main pattern which is more interesting than just plain colour. This type of long stool, running the length of the bed, provides useful extra seating and makes a pleasing addition to the bed itself.

ALCOVE BEDS

There is something incredibly seductive and inviting about alcove beds. They seem to beckon you in, accompanied by lover or book, for a time of utterly private indulgence. The only decision is whether to release the tie-backs and let the curtains hide you.

To create an alcove all you really need is a recess the width of a double wardrobe in which to put the bed; this could be devised by using the space on either side of the bed for cupboards. In that way, you could get away with minimal furniture.

In the picture on the left, a secluded retreat has been created by using nothing more than a few tacks and several metres of fabric. For lining the inside of the alcove a dark mottled cotton chintz has been draped in loose panels to create swags, while the sleigh bed is covered in the same fabric. For the outer curtaining, a shaded striped cotton forms three overlapping swags and tied back curtains. However, instead of using conventional silk cording to trim the top of the swags and for the tie-backs, the designer has simply twisted lengths of the dark chintz and the striped fabric together to cover the tacks used to hold the swags.

Another clever detail is the striped trimming on the bedlinen, which picks up the tones and pattern of the curtaining. The softly marbled linen also works to unite the strong contrasts in the colour scheme. The only departure from the soft luxuriance of the folds and swags is the bedside table, with its tailored box-pleated cover and dark red piping, matching that on the bed.

Here, rich autumnal tones have been chosen to enhance the ormolu-mounted French Empire furniture. What makes the alcove drapery so distinctive is the swagged, fringed and tasselled valance. It gives focus to the bed and is in keeping with the style of the room.

Probably the finest trimmings were made in the late seventeenth and early eighteenth centuries. They were not only produced commercially but also made at home by noblewomen as a useful and agreeable pastime – even George III's wife, Queen Charlotte, had a frame for making fringe. But alas, the fashion faded and today trimmings are rarely used effectively in a room scheme.

There are signs, however, that we are due for a revival. Here, a co-ordinating range of trimmings has made the decorator's job easy – double tie-backs are used as a finishing touch to the valance, which is edged, as are the curtains, with plain bullion; single fan edging is used to finish the footstool.

The alcove itself has been papered in the striped floral co-ordinate of the fabric, which has wisely not been used on the main walls of the room, but confined to the alcove. The soft furnishings have some interesting touches – note the outline quilting on the bedspread and the diagonal quilting of the plain silk cushions. (For other cushion treatments, see pages 158–159.) Period details include the use of flat picot braid to hang prints and a light switch in the form of a bell pull.

A detail of the valance, showing how the cord is knotted round "ears" of chintz which have been stiffened with buckram to make them stand up.

AN ATTIC RETREAT

A bedroom under the eaves of a country cottage might not seem the most obvious place for a four-poster bed, but in the past four-posters were not restricted to grand settings. Remarkably versatile pieces of furniture, they varied from sumptuous brocade-hung state beds to quite modest affairs, with curtains serving simply to cut out draughts and light.

In this room there is insufficient space above the window to allow for a practical curtain treatment and so simple wooden shutters have been used. For this reason the four-poster has real, not dress, curtains full enough to draw right round the bed and exclude daylight.

The bed has a plain putty-coloured timber frame, in keeping with the paler roof beams. The curtains are in a large-scale print of

rampant vegetation in unusually moody tones of dark blue on beige. Both curtains and canopy are lined in raspberry, a tone picked up in the tablecloth with a different floral print. The same patterned fabric covers the sofa at the foot of the bed, enlivened by cushions in mottled beige, matching the wallpaper. Although plain white walls or small flowery sprigs are what one sees only too often in cottage bedrooms, the choice of this wall-covering demonstrates the advantages of an all-over textural pattern: concealment of the inevitable unevenness of old plaster, and a feeling of warmth and comfort which would be denied by stark white.

This room shows how even in a small area different patterns and textures can live in harmony if the component colours are co-ordinated carefully.

BATHROOMS

LIEUX A L'ANGLAISE

No other nationality is quite so good as the British at the comfortable bathroom. In fact the English are generally credited with inventing the whole concept of a separate room for the bath. When bathing was not considered an entirely necessary activity in France in the eighteenth century, bathrooms – something of a rarity – were sometimes known as *'lieux à l'anglaise'* (and from the abbreviated *'lieux'* came our coy appellation of 'loo').

Presented with the greatest luxury of all – space – the owners of this bathroom (*left*) have managed to make it look as if the room has simply evolved over the years, with its pictures, furniture and knick-knacks. The sanitary fittings are reconditioned Edwardian originals and charmingly old-fashioned trellis and floral stripe cotton curtains are kept in place in the simplest possible manner: they are tied on to brass rings.

There is no reason why modesty should prevail in bathroom decor – if you have elegant windows (*below left*) then dress them accordingly. Draped curtains, first popularized in France in the eighteenth century, have had an immense revival in the last few years, threatening to eclipse completely the now rather overused festoon blind. In the wrong hands they can, however, be disastrous: the secret is not to skimp with materials, and, unless you are or have an excellent curtain-maker, to stick to a simple design. Although these curtains look ambitious they are in fact a fairly basic construction: over the curtain is draped a swag of fabric with a tail hanging down at either end. The curtains might have looked a little overdressed in an otherwise featureless room, so a wallpaper border imitating an architectural frieze has been doubled up to create a *trompe l'oeil* cornice (*below right*). Applying the same border above the skirting board neatly frames the room.

MARBLE REAL AND FALSE

Though predominantly pink and cream, the marbled walls of the bathroom opposite have a hint of grey, and a softly gathered gauzy blind is edged in a very dark charcoal stippled cotton. This dark zig-zag edging serves to balance the slab of black marble surrounding the basins in an otherwise pastel room. Allied with the black marble, the gleaming chrome taps, large expanse of mirror and chrome and frosted glass wall lights give a glamorous, slightly Thirties look.

It takes only the simplest of decorating solutions to give a narrow bathroom (*above*) airs and graces. A mirrored wall completely enclosing the bath instantly seems to enlarge

the space, and the suggestion of a partition in the form of a painted arch above the bath creates the sense of a separate bathing area. Painted *faux marbre* walls – the marbling extends down over the skirting board, up over the cornice and along the bath panel for a *trompe l'oeil* effect – provide the opulence of marble without the expense. But what lifts the whole room out of the ordinary is the window treatment: a loosely-woven linen, edged with pompom fringe, is a more interesting alternative to traditional sheers, perfect for simple asymmetrical drapes like this – a style that found its way from France to Sweden in the 1820s and still looks fresh and charming today.

Marble is the most luxurious of surface materials, but whether it's real, as a basin surround, or painted, as a finish for walls and woodwork, it is best used to create a feeling of understated elegance (above and right) rather than showy opulence. It needs to be softened by textiles – rugs, curtains or blinds, as here – to avoid making the room too cold.

BATHED IN TRADITION

When a room has a character of its own it is preferable to be led by it rather than impose an arbitrary alien design. With the sloping ceiling and country feel of this cottage bathroom (*right*) a modern panelled bath would look totally out of place, but a free-standing bath and basin and Edwardian-style brass fittings are perfect. Matt-painted tongue-and-groove wood to dado height, to match the grey of the bath's exterior, has a suitably rustic air. Ornithological prints carefully grouped below the sloping ceiling make an attractive finishing touch.

Another bathroom in the same cottage has the same rustic charm (*below*). The original exposed beams are painted in a pale putty colour, as a subtler, less intrusive contrast with the white ceiling than the traditional black. The same grey-painted boarding has been used, allied here with floral sprigged paper. Above the generously-sized, old-fashioned wash basin the simple mirror is surmounted (as in the other picture) by a specially made wooden cornice to conceal and shade a modern strip light, which, though thoroughly practical, would not be in keeping with a traditional interior.

CABINETS DE BAIN

Even the most box-like, windowless city bathroom can be given atmosphere and character (*left*). Here a tiled recess has been created for the bath and low-voltage lighting in the lowered ceiling gives a diffused light. Because a completely tiled room was felt to be too clinical, the owners chose a stippled blue-grey wallpaper for the walls outside the recess. (Wallpaper in bathrooms is not such a modern innovation as might be supposed: Madame de Pompadour was noted to have chosen a flock wallpaper for her *cabinet de bain*.) A marble wash-stand with a Minton-tiled back and a mahogany-framed basin hark back to solid Victorian comfort, while modern prints and an inlaid Indo-Portuguese mirror add individuality.

Pictures are again a distinguishing personal feature in this tiny bathroom (*below*). Nineteenth-century engravings of birds and monkeys, uniformly framed in gilt, are hung over the bath within panels made simply from moulding painted in a contrasting colour to the wall. Old-fashioned brass fittings contribute to the reassuringly traditional atmosphere.

Once you have the interior architecture right, it is the decorative details that make a bathroom into a temple of ablutions. Here, a collection of seashell-shaped plates decorates the basin alcove (*above*) and also works well with the rosa vinca marble surround, while a grouping of stones and fossils from the seashore fills a glass bowl on the window sill. These allusions to watery places have been popular ever since bathrooms were in common usage: as early as the late seventeenth century there were numerous papers featuring waterside motifs, ranging from the waterfalls and lakesides of oriental papers to the fountains and cherubs of the French master Jean-Baptiste Réveillon.

Another view (*right*) of the same bathroom shows the elegant window treatment. A dress curtain of unlined white silk is arranged as a swag with tails, fixed with large bows. Behind it is a plain net. White silk has the rare quality of enhancing daylight and so is a suitable, if unusually luxurious, choice for the dark alcove.

DESIGN DETAIL

CHAIRS

Modern loose covers derive from case covers, used from the seventeenth century onwards to protect costly and delicate fabrics from wear as well as light and dust. The material most commonly used was calico, often overprinted with large checks or stripes. It seems that in grand houses the covers were removed only on special occasions – a practice which explains their increasing decorativeness, to the point when, as today, they became the permanent covering for chairs and sofas.

These high-backed dining chairs (*opposite*) have an eighteenth-century air in their summer covers of palest grey mottled chintz. They have a sky-blue trim – a flat, finely pinked ruffle at the back and sides, and neat edging, extended to make ties, at the base.

Small occasional chairs covered in a weave with a vine-leaf motif are given individuality and stylishness by unusual finishing touches (*above*). Heavy rope tassels decorate the scroll backs and rows of brass studs are used not merely to finish the lower edge, but to make a scalloped line around the base.

Glazed chintz in a bold modern print has been used to cover a set of low-backed dining chairs (*above*). An over-long skirt is gathered round the base of the chair and there is a ruched and piped band along the top. Extra fullness at the back is caught in by bows with long ties; these are lined in deep purple to match one of the colours in the chintz.

SIDE TABLES

Skirted side tables are an excellent way of bringing colour and pattern into a room, as well as providing a surface on which to arrange objects in that artful placement known to decorators as a 'tablescape'. And while a dressed table always lends a comfortable, finished air to a room, it is one of the easiest decorating devices, as the table itself can be made exactly to the size and shape required.

Skirting a table can satisfy longings for fabrics that are too extravagant or bold for large-scale upholstery – and of course the possibilities of style are endless, as these pictures show.

In the large picture opposite, a console table in an alcove is framed by full-length curtains in glazed chintz, their vertical floral bands alternating with trellis. The tabletop is covered in the same fabric pulled up in symmetrical ruched swags which are secured at the middle and corners with rosettes, in keeping with the flowery theme. The underskirt is dark green, picked up by the green malachite painted finish of the twin lamp bases. A co-ordinating wallpaper with a Gothic motif makes a good background both to the nineteenth-century water-colour and to the decorative objects on the table.

The small picture below shows a simple but opulent tablecloth made from a heavy tapestry weave fabric with thick bullion fringe as a trim. The fabric is carefully cut to show off the broad stripes to advantage; its sophisticated design of leopard spots allied with floral panels adds a modern twist to a traditional style.

More often associated with frilly feminine rooms, skirted tables can work just as effectively in adding a soft, fluid touch to a scheme with simple clean-cut lines (*above*). Here a large sculptural drape of cloth is gently waisted with a thick cord and tassels; a deliberately over-long drop allows the heavy fabric to pool gently on to the floor. Just visible is the edge of the lining, which is in brighter blue to match the tassels; lining a tablecloth is not essential, but adds weight to make it hang well and gives a more finished look when, as here, the underside is likely to be seen.

This carefully casual style demands a certain informality in the arrangements of the objects on top: too much neatness and symmetry would spoil the effect. The unfussy arrangement of books, dried flowers and lamp perfectly complements the table's draped simplicity.

The combination of a striped fabric and an octagonal table demands special attention to pattern-matching (*below*). The cloth is cut into eight segments to highlight the shape of the table, and the converging stripes form an intriguing pattern of chevrons. Breaking up strong geometric designs in such a way allows

them to be used elsewhere in a room as well – for curtains and upholstery, perhaps – without the total effect becoming overpowering.

Small objects are best displayed on a table because you look down on it; seen from the side on a mantelpiece they hide each other from view. So every collector should have a table like this (*above*) for displaying favourite treasures. The design of a tablescape is a minor art form: the array can be a miniature museum, grouping kindred objects by form, function or design, and each display can make its own rules, creating its own tiny universe.

Here a darker fabric has been chosen for the underskirt – an African-inspired blue weave – and a square of lighter-coloured fabric with a smaller pattern for the top. A deep fringe in a surprising but successful choice of colours calls attention to the table's display.

A top cloth perfectly tailored to fit the octagonal table (*below*) has an arresting zigzag hem detail that was suggested by the large diamonds of the plaid. The gathered skirt is further accentuated by wide blue piping picking up the blues of both the plaid and the plain underskirt.

CUSHIONS

Before including cushions in a scheme the thoughtful decorator will consider their practical purpose: first, do they make seating more comfortable? Secondly, will the piece of furniture they are intended for really look better with them? If so, they should be planned as an integral part of the room, so that they add colour, pattern and texture in a convincing way. What should be avoided is the temptation to use up odd pieces of fabric for a fussy pile of small, non-functional scatter cushions – cushions should be large and interesting enough to add to the whole effect.

There are practical considerations that will determine how the cushion looks and feels, the most important being the choice of stuffing. Feathers are the best choice – obtainable in different grades of softness, they give a comfortable, lived-in look and last for years. The quantity of stuffing used is also critical: while squab cushions on dining chairs need less dense padding, larger cushions, on a sofa for instance, should be well-packed and firm so that they give proper support and retain their shape.

Decoration with suitable trimmings adds greatly to the finished appearance of cushions. Traditional trimmings made from natural fibres are increasingly difficult to obtain, but are generally preferable to man-made fibre imitations, which neither wear so well nor fade so gracefully. Because few haberdashers or upholsterers today know the names and correct use of the various types of trimming, they are often used inappropriately. In fact, all the classic trimmings have been developed over many years for particular purposes, so it is possible to be quite specific about their function.

Of the basic styles, looped ruche is often used on upholstery for concealing tacks but is good for finishing cushions, adding definition and substance (1). Flat, tape-like braids are useful decoration in their own right: broad bands of large picot braid look effective against a background of crushed velvet (4).

Rope, coiled to combine two or three colours, makes a good accent or edging on relatively plain fabrics (4 and 11). Fringes, plain and fan-topped, add textural variety, and, used for contrast to pick up a colour in the cushion fabric, are much more striking than self-piped edges (7 and 5).

The picture shows a variety of ideas for cushion styles and trims: camellia motifs appliquéd to a toning shagreen print, bordered with a looped ruche trim (1); a tapestry weave fabric, its plain hem marked by a thick line of stitching and finished at the outer edge with fine piping (2); geometric patchwork using three colourways of glazed chintz edged with plain self-piping (3); crushed velvet with bands of wide picot braid finished with rope (4); a triangular cushion in glazed chintz edged in plain fringe which again picks up a dominant colour in the fabric (5); a round cushion in a modern print with a scalloped and gathered border (6); a plaid design outline-quilted along the diagonal lattice bands and edged with plain fringe toning with the main colour (7); quilted silk with fine rouleau piping (8); Art Deco-inspired cut velvet with a thick rouleau trim of gathered silk to make an interesting and opulent combination of textures (9); zigzag motifs cut out and appliquéd to a co-ordinating stippled fabric, the padded hem finished with contrast piping (10); a dark tapestry weave with a flat hem decorated by rope knotted at the corners (11); a pale stippled fabric wrapped in an outer cover of patterned glazed chintz with plain binding that extends to form ties (12); striped silk cut diagonally, with the stripes used vertically for the frill (13); a blue silk square quilted on the diagonal with contrast piping (14).

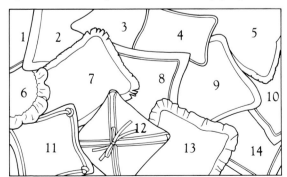

LAMPSHADES

Lamps and lampshades are too often the poor relations in a decorative scheme, added as an afterthought without much consideration as to how well they will complement their surroundings. Shown here are some ideas for lampshade treatments chosen with particular settings in mind.

The picture on the right is an intriguing demonstration of how objects spanning four

centuries and as many countries can be harmoniously combined. A hand-painted caned French bergère chair with a striped silk cushion stands beside an inlaid Indo-Portuguese table with an English willow bowl and two late Georgian mahogany candlestick lamps. To tie them in with the setting, the shades, in the same colour as the wallpaper ground behind, have been stencilled with an enlarged version of the paper's flower motif.

This pair of spattered dark green ceramic lamp bases *(above)* have coolie shades – the shape traditionally used to balance tall thin candlestick bases. Pleated shades can look very formal in silk, but here, in flowered chintz, they are pretty and informal. A further softening touch is the fan edge braid trim.

A tall telescoping brass candlestick lamp gives a generous spill of light for reading by in a quiet corner *(left)*. A fabric with a design of owl feathers has been chosen for the lampshade, the pattern merging in a soft mottled effect and the colours echoing the terracotta walls and the hints of muted blue in the tapestry-covered cushions.

A more lavish setting (*above*) is an exercise in total co-ordination. Striped flowered chintz in blue and amber is matched with blue paper, blue silk curtains edged with the chintz and an amber silk festoon blind. To preserve the unity of the scheme, a lampshade has been made from the chintz, carefully pleated to preserve the striped effect. The lamp base co-ordinates as well – it is spattered in the same colours, but in slightly darker, duller tones, in order not to compete with the shade.

A pair of identical lamps and shades (*below*) look equally good in different colourways. On the left, an Empire shade is made from a tortoiseshell-patterned paper in shades of blue, concertina-pleated and banded top and bottom with the same paper in a paler tone. It tops a highly glazed base in matching speckled blue. Beside it, a Carlton ware compote holds silken fruit. The lamp on the right has a shade in burgundy and red edged with apricot, while the base is spattered in the same tones.

A nineteenth-century brass reading lamp with a black enamelled base has been given an unusual and romantic shade design to enliven its sombre setting *(above)*. Usually these lamps are seen with glass shades, but here a plain pleated shade has been topped with a reefed 'skirt' in wine-red chintz, its rich, jewel-like colours in keeping with the Victorians' love of deep tones.

An unusual cylindrical glass lamp base depicting a Chinese merchant was the point of departure for this lampshade treatment *(below left)*. The pleated black silk coolie shade is trimmed with dull gold ribbon to accentuate the Chinese theme and pick up the gold of the base.

Nothing makes a more dramatic impression than black – and no black is deeper or richer than black lacquer. Here *(below right)* the glossy urn lamp base and shade are set in front of a red glazed chintz curtain. Flower motifs have been cut out from the chintz and mounted on the shade for perfect co-ordination.

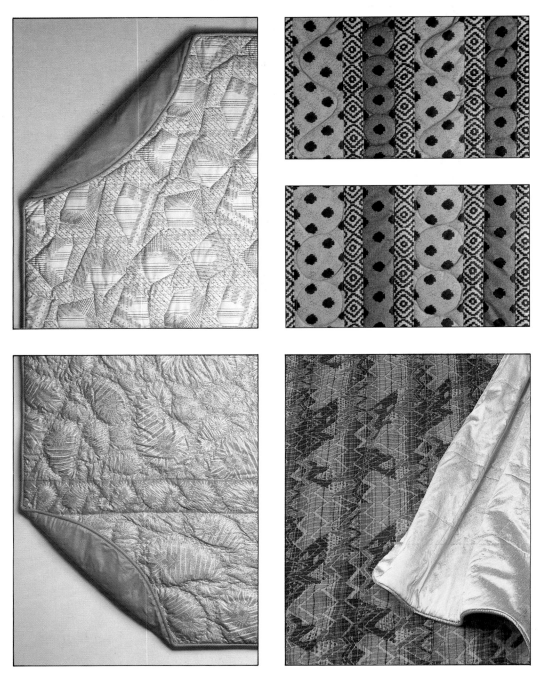

Top left: *Outline quilting in single chain stitch following the irregular geometric shapes of the pattern.* Top right: *Raised Italian quilting edging each vertical ochre stripe to produce a 'channelled' effect; within the spotted pink stripes a stitched line forms an S-shape in the top panel, circular shapes below.* Bottom left: *More complicated outline quilting, showing how an intricate design can be defined to produce a rich effect; the quilt has been jumbo-piped at the perimeter in the same fabric used for the underside.* Bottom right: *A luxurious throw in rich Art Deco-inspired cut velvet backed with shot silk. It can be used on either side and would look lavish and dramatic flung over a sofa as well as on a bed.*

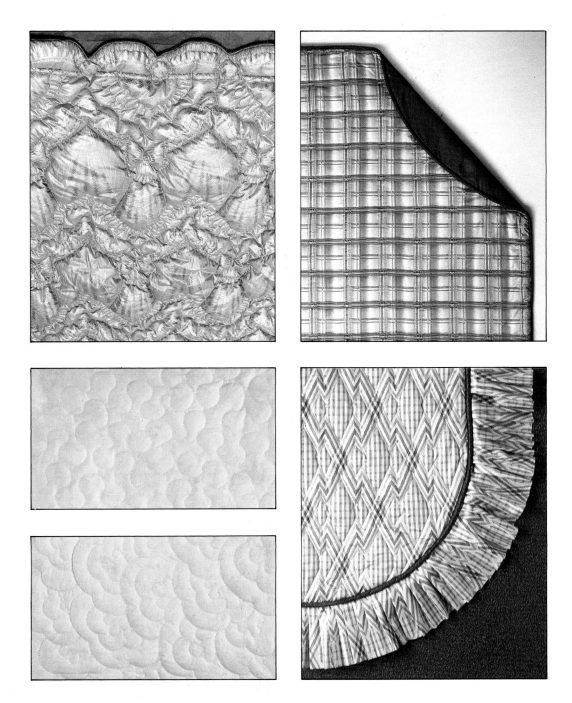

Top left: *A glazed chintz outline-quilted round the intricate shell design. The piped scalloped edge follows the pattern.* Top right: *Italian quilting, used this time to pick out and emphasize the violet stripe in the checked fabric – note that the same shade of violet has been used to pipe and back the quilt.* Bottom left: *A softly stippled fabric enhanced by two types of machine quilting: at the top, a random 'vermicelli' squiggle; at the bottom, a freestyle design of overlapping scallops. Both of these were achieved with a pre-set machine stitch.* Bottom right: *Outline quilting in single chain stitch following the motif in the fabric. The quilt has been edged with a knife-pleated frill in the same fabric, with the join concealed by a line of jumbo piping.*

SCREENS

Folding panel screens (as opposed to cheval or pole screens used as heat shields in front of fireplaces or to mask empty hearths in summer) were intended to reduce draughts. This purpose did not prevent their being treated as decorative pieces of furniture, however, and from as early as the sixteenth century there are records of screens of all shapes and sizes made from leather, wicker, painted cloth and embroidered fabric.

In the seventeenth and eighteenth centuries oriental screens became popular when lacquer panels were imported in considerable quantities by the East India Company. Sometimes several panels –

Above: This screen is covered in wallpaper resembling dragged paintwork in two contrasting colours. The inner panels are outlined in a border paper, mitred at the corners and also used along the screen's outer edges.

Right: A simple mahogany-edged screen with small round feet has each face covered in a different woven fabric: for the back a stripe and for the front a zigzag, both sides edged in wide picot braid.

occasionally up to a dozen – were linked to produce what were effectively quite large movable partitions. Later in the eighteenth century smaller screens came back into favour, often with two wooden frames mounted on plain legs. The frame itself might be ornamental, with carved crests or corner brackets, but usually the panels themselves were considered the chief decorative element.

Fabric and paper were the materials most often used for the panels. The fabric might be tapestry, satin or embroidered wool or linen; continuing the oriental vogue, silk panels painted with Chinese scenes were made especially for use on screens. Paper panels with similar designs were also available; alternatively, paper screens might feature water-colour paintings or mezzotints.

But it was in the nineteenth century that folding screens reached their pinnacle of popularity. In the Victorian drawing room they were as ubiquitous as footstools. Some

Above: These panels have been edged in red lacquer to complement the patterned chintz with its images of oriental porcelain – a modern re-creation of the lacquer screens in the seventeenth and eighteenth centuries.

Above: A three-panel mahogany screen with removable fabric panels, and topped by turned acorns. The two fabrics have been sewn together with a casing at the top and bottom of each panel to allow a rod to be inserted.

were made of papier mâché, some were gilded, others were embellished with Berlin work or other fashionable stitchery, or had glass panels set in rococo frames, but in whatever form all were highly decorative as well as functional. Some were supplied with blank panels to display prints or family photographs, and a perennial favourite was the scrapwork screen. These were made from scraps carefully cut out of books and journals, glued to paper or fabric panels and varnished.

Today screens are no longer needed as draught shields but instead can act as room-dividers, can hide untidy corners or unsightly views and generally offer infinite possibilities for adding height to a furniture grouping, and colour and texture to a room. They can be created from fabric-covered frames, joined with two-way screen hinges, or from plain panels which are then painted or papered.

Above: A screen made entirely from wallpaper, with a rosy strié paper background, and trompe l'oeil *panels of co-ordinating apricot strié edged with a wallpaper border. Here the top three panels are used to display hand-coloured architectural designs in authentic eighteenth-century fashion.*

Above: A finely striped brown fabric is used for a four-fold screen, its panels topped with Gothic arches and edged with brass tacks.

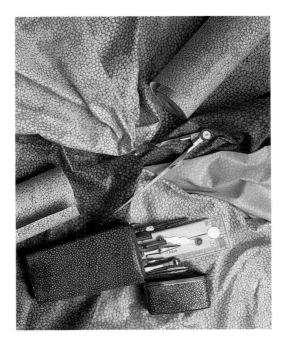

CREDITS

FABRIC AND WALLPAPER DETAILS

Endpapers: Painter/Tortoiseshell WT015.

Pages 2–3: as pages 82–83.

Pages 4–5: as pages 92–94.

Page 6: Painter Collection.

Page 9: Tamesa Weaves Collection.

Pages 10–11: wallpapers Siena WS423/ WS420; borders BS159A/BS160E; curtain Siena FS420.

Page 12: wallpaper Regatta WR38; curtain Sirius F198A.

Page 13: wallpaper Regatta WR23.

Pages 14–15: wallpaper Regatta WR21.

Page 16: borders: Sirius BSIR10/BSIR07.

Page 17: border: Sirius BSIR/17.

Pages 18–19: wallpaper: Plains/Nuage W10; chairs Sirius/Eclipse F197C.

Page 20: wallpaper Patina/Patchgrain BF06.

Page 21: wallpaper Arcadia/Pansy Stripe W200C; curtains Arcadia/Pansy Stripe F200B; inner curtain Taffeta Silk 117; tablecloth Genoa 09.

Pages 22–23: wallpaper China/Crocus Trellis W222A; fabric China/Crocus Trellis F222A; pink cushion Shagreen FSH10.

Page 24: wallpaper Shagreen WSH09; curtains, tablecloth Shagreen FSH09.

Page 25: wallpaper Siena WS410; swag Siena FS420, bows FS418.

Pages 26–27: wallpaper Regatta WR26; curtains Griffin 03; window seat cushion Villandry 02.

Page 28: (*top*) curtains Sirius/Quasar F191D; window seat cushion, inner curtains Tamesa Silk/Carmen 01. (*Below*) curtains Tamesa Silk/Carmen 02/09; cushion Malmaison 02.

Page 29: wallpaper Plains/Nuage W10; curtains Puff 02; window seat cushion Griffin 04; patchwork cushion Puff 02/03; tablecloth Plains/Nuage F10.

Pages 30–31: wallpaper Arcadia/Camellia Ribbon W201D; fabric Arcadia/Camellia Ribbon F201D.

Page 32: walls Regatta FR61; ceiling, sofa, tablecloth Regatta FR51.

Page 33: wallpaper Pergola/Parrot Tulips W143D; sofa Pergola/Parrot Tulips F143D.

Pages 34–37: wallpaper Shagreen WSH03; border Shagreen WSH05; curtains, plaid armchair Sirius/Quasar F191B; sofas Stippleglaze STGL20, trim STGL13; ottoman Pansy Stripe 01.

Pages 38–39: wallpaper China/Mina Screen W223A; fabric China/Ming Screen F223A; cushions Genoa 01/02; floor Malmaison 01.

Pages 40–41: wallpaper Sirius/Saturn WSIR14, border BSIR09; curtains, sofa Sirius/Saturn F192C; cushions, tablecloth, ottoman Sirius/Stippleglaze STGL09/06.

Page 42: (*top*) wallpaper Sirius WSIR53; curtains Sirius/Nebula F198A. (*Below*) Arcadia/Pansy Stripe F200A.

Page 43: wallpaper Regatta WR10; sofa, ottoman, blind Regatta FR62; curtains Regatta FR52.

Pages 44–45: wallpaper Sunstitch WWS09; sofa Shagreen FSH01.

Pages 46–47: wallpaper Sirius/Omega WSIR39, border BSIR18; fabric Sirius/ Omega F195E; blind Sirius/Stippleglaze STGL22; cushions STGL22/25.

Page 48: blind, ottoman Sahara/Ikali 01; curtains, pelmet, cushions Sahara/Kiffa 01; sofa, pelmet inserts Sahara/Safi 02.

Page 49: curtains, pelmet, cabinets Sahara/ Ikali 06; pelmet contrast squares Sahara/ Safi 02; blind Sahara/Kiffa 06.

Pages 50–51: wallpaper Siena WS403; curtains Regatta FR54; sofas Weaves/Aspen 01; chair Nuage FN127.

Pages 52–53: wallpaper Floribunda WF08; sofa, chair Sahara/Safi 11; ottoman, cushions Pansy Stripe 01.

Page 54: curtains Darkwood/Bramble F180C, trim Stippleglaze STGL18; chair Siena FS401.

Page 55: wallpaper Regatta WR12; curtains Regatta FR53; sofa Sunstitch FWS23.

Pages 56–57: wall fabric Arcadia/Camellia Ribbon F201A; chair Sunstitch FWS22.

Page 58: curtains Taffeta 103, lining 109; sofa Puff 04; cushions Villandry 04/Rambouillet 02; tablecloth Genoa 07.

Page 59: wallpaper Floribunda/Rose Ribbon WF11; tablecloth Sirius/Saturn F192A, undercloth Genoa 08.

Pages 60–61: fabric Botanica/Sissinghurst F173A.

Pages 62–63: wallpaper Siena WS413; blinds Nuage F18, trim FN138; ottoman Stippleglaze STGL20.

Pages 64–65: wallpaper Arcadia/Geranium W204E; curtains, sofa Arcadia/Geranium F204E; ottoman Malmaison 03; armchair Shagreen FSH12.

Pages 66–67: wallpapers Arcadia/Pansy Stripe W200C/W0128; fabric Arcadia/Pansy Stripe F200C; upholstery Genoa 08/09; lamps LA02, shades LS19; carpet Spice/Cayenne 4710.

Pages 68–69: wallpaper Sirius WSIR39; curtains Tamesa Silk Royalty 07; swags Sirius/Omega F195E.

Page 70: curtains Stippleglaze STGL19, bows STGL02.

Page 71: Tamesa Weaves Collection.

Pages 72–73: curtains Tamesa Silk Royalty 07.

Pages 74–75: wallpaper China/Imari Vases W224A; fabric China/Imari Vases F224A.

Pages 76–77: wallpaper Regatta WR17; curtains Darkwood F180C, lining Stippleglaze STGL12.

Pages 78–79: fabric Pergola/Parrot Tulips F143D.

Pages 80–81: wallpapers Arcadia/Wild Poppy W203D/W0117, border BA06; curtain, tablecloth Arcadia/Wild Poppy F203D; lining, undercloth Stippleglaze STGL13.

Pages 82–84: fabric Botanica/Albert F170C; chairs Sunstitch FWS09.

Page 85: Petitpoint Collection.

Page 86: wallpaper Regatta WR21; curtains, chair Regatta FR55; stool, window seat Regatta FR65.

Page 87: curtains Regatta FR551; chairs, pelmet trim Regatta FR61.

Pages 88–89: wallpaper Sirius WSIR05, border BSIR01; curtains Sirius/Scintilla F190A; chair Sirius/Meteor F196D; trim Stippleglaze STGL13/19.

Pages 90–91: wallpaper Arcadia/Geranium W204A; pelmet, chair Arcadia/Geranium F204A; curtains Tamesa Silk Taffeta 12; cushions Taffeta 109/112; lamp LA05, shade Taffeta 109.

Pages 92–94: wallpaper Floribunda WF11; curtains China/Fishing Scene F221D; desk chair cushion Tamesa Silk/Seraglio 07; upholstery Malmaison 02.

Page 95: Stippleglaze Collection.

Pages 96–99: table runners, cushions Regatta FR58; curtain Tamesa Weave/Lyric 07.

Pages 100–101: wallpaper Sirius WSIR29, border BSIR15; curtains Sirius/Quasar F191A.

Pages 102–103: wallpaper Siena WS413,

ADDRESSES

HEAD OFFICE

OSBORNE & LITTLE plc
49 Temperley Road
London SW12 8QE
Tel: 01-675 2255

SHOWROOMS

OSBORNE & LITTLE plc
304 King's Road
London SW3 5UH
Tel: 01-352 1456/7/8

OSBORNE & LITTLE plc
43 Conduit Street
London W1R 9FB
Tel: 01-494 2307/8/9

OSBORNE & LITTLE plc
39 Queen Street
Edinburgh EH2 3NH
Tel: 031-226 3110

OSBORNE & LITTLE plc
Barton Arcade
Deansgate
Manchester M3 2AZ
Tel: 061-834 0475

USA

HEAD OFFICE

OSBORNE & LITTLE
65 Commerce Road
Stamford
CT 06902

SHOWROOM

OSBORNE & LITTLE
D & D Building
Suite 1503N
979 Third Avenue
New York
N.Y. 10022

ACKNOWLEDGEMENTS

Photographs taken by the following:

FRITZ VON DER SCHULENBURG: pages 2–3, 12–13, 19 (by permission of *House & Garden*, Condé Nast Publications Ltd), 20, 24–25 (owner The Hon Mrs Charmian Stirling, from *The Englishwoman's Garden*, published by Chatto & Windus), 26–27, 28 (top), 29, 36–37 (by permission of *House & Garden*), 44–45, 52–53, 64–65, 72–73 (owner Lady McAlpine, by permission of *The World of Interiors*, Pharos Publications Ltd), 76–77, 87, 92–94, 96–99, 104–105 (by permission of *House & Garden*), 106–107 (owner Mrs Adam Loxton-Peacock), 108, 110–113, 114–115, 119 (by permission of *House & Garden*), 122–123 (owner Lady Sarah Aspinall, from *The Englishwoman's Bedroom*, published by Chatto & Windus), 132–133 (owner Mrs Adam Loxton-Peacock), 140, 143, 144 (owner Mrs Adam Loxton-Peacock), 145, 146–147, 148–149 (large picture by permission of *House & Garden*), 150, 156–157, 164 (bottom right), 165 (top left), 174–175.

CHARLES SETTRINGTON: 6, 9, 10–11, 22–23, 38, 41, 47, 55, 60–61, 66–67, 71, 74–75, 80–81, 86, 89, 90–91, 95, 109, 117, 120–121, 125, 128, 134–135, 136–139, 141, 151.

MARTIN HILL: pages 10, 16–17, 18, 28 (bottom), 30–31, 34–35, 39, 40, 42, 46, 48–49, 54–55, 58–59, 62–63, 68–69, 70, 88, 100–101 (owner Sarah Brown), 102, 116, 118, 124, 129, 130–131, 152 (top), 153, 154–155, 156 (bottom), 157 (bottom), 160–163, 164 (top, left and right; bottom left), 165 (top right; bottom left and right), 166–168.

ANDREAS VON EINSIEDEL: pages 4–5, 50–51, 82–84, 126–127 (all by permission of *Madame* magazine).

STEPHEN HAYWARD: pages 14–15, 43, 142.

JAMES MORTIMER: pages 78–79 (interior designer Victoria Waymouth, Rain Interiors; by permission of *The World of Interiors*).

STANLI OPPERMAN: pages 158–159.

TREVOR RICHARDS: pages 56–57 (by permission of *Homes & Gardens*, IPC Magazines Ltd).

PETER WILLIAMS: page 33.